THE HARRY POTTER BIBLE STUDY

Enjoying God Through the Final Four
Harry Potter Movies

JARED MOORE

The Harry Potter Bible Study: Enjoying God Through the Final Four Harry Potter Movies

Copyright © 2011 Jared Moore

All rights reserved. No part of this publication may be reproduced, stored in a retrieval system, or transmitted in any form by any means, electronic, mechanical, photocopy, recording, or otherwise, without the prior permission of the publisher, except as provided for by USA copyright law.

Scripture quotations are from The Holy Bible, English Standard Version® (ESV®), copyright © 2001 by Crossway, a publishing ministry of Good News Publishers. Used by permission. All rights reserved.

Cover picture: Amber Moore

All emphases in quotations have been added by the author.

This book has not been prepared, approved, or licensed by any person or entity that created, published, or produced the Harry Potter books, movies, or related properties.

ISBN: 1466433604
ISBN-13: 978-1466433601

DEDICATION

To

Amber with great love and appreciation for your grace and faithfulness. I love you deeply. To Caden and Ava, daddy's buddies. Remember, God gave you life for the purpose of enjoying Him, but, due to your sin, you can only enjoy Him through recognizing His fingerprints in creation in light of Scripture and His Son Jesus Christ's redeeming work. Repent and believe the gospel.

CONTENTS

	ACKNOWLEDGMENTS	i
	INTRODUCTION	1
1	HOW TO ENJOY GOD THROUGH HARRY POTTER	19
2	EVIL ELEMENTS PRESENT IN THE HARRY POTTER SERIES	29
3	HARRY POTTER AND THE ORDER OF THE PHOENIX	37
4	HARRY POTTER AND THE HALF-BLOOD PRINCE	53
5	HARRY POTTER AND THE DEATHLY HALLOWS – PART 1	71
6	HARRY POTTER AND THE DEATHLY HALLOWS – PART 2	89
	APPENDIX 1: IN FAVOR OF CHRISTIANS WATCHING SCARY MOVIES	107
	BIBLIOGRAPHY	111
	SCRIPTURE INDEX	113

INTRODUCTION

Before You Begin

Items Needed.
- Bible
- TV
- VHS, DVD, or Blu-Ray Player
- *Harry Potter and the Order of the Phoenix* Movie
- *Harry Potter and the Half-Blood Prince* Movie
- *Harry Potter and the Deathly Hallows - Part 1* Movie
- *Harry Potter and the Deathly Hallows - Part 2* Movie

What This Book Is And What This Book Is Not. This book is a Bible study based on interacting with primarily the final four *Harry Potter* movies, not the books. But, since the movies and books are close in their substance, you may use this study to interact with the final three *Harry Potter* books (there were eight movies, but only seven books), as well. This study is more of an overview examination of these *Harry Potter* movies instead of an exhaustive examination. Since each chapter is meant to be read in one sitting, it was impossible to exhaustively examine every subtle detail of

Harry Potter. I have instead tried to provide enough insight into this series to help train the youngest to the eldest learner concerning how Christians should interact with pop culture. My goal is for readers to gain enough understanding of how to exercise a Christian view of the world in their daily lives, so that they may participate in the various "truth and lie webs" produced by God's fallen image-bearers without becoming entangled in sin.

Read Before You Watch. If you have already seen the movies, I still suggest you begin this study before rewatching the movies. Before you watch *Harry Potter and the Order of the Phoenix* (2007), *Harry Potter and the Half-Blood Prince* (2009), *Harry Potter and the Deathly Hallows - Part 1* (2010) and *Harry Potter and the Deathly Hallows - Part 2* (2011), read Chapters 1 and 2. These chapters, along with this introduction, will help prepare you to engage these *Harry Potter* movies or books in a distinctly Christian manner, a manner which will glorify God as you seek to reveal how the *Harry Potter* series, along with all humans involved in creating it, exist in our God's world.

Watch Before You Read. Before you read Chapters 3-6, watch the movie that has the same name as the title of the chapter. You can buy or rent these movies online or at your local video store. Watching each movie prior to reading its subsequent chapter is important because each chapter contains spoilers! You will be sorely disappointed if you read this book before you watch these movies.

How to Use This Bible Study

Timestamps. Because this Bible study is primarily interacting with the *Harry Potter* movies, I have provided timestamps—00:00:00—i.e. hours:minutes:seconds. These numbers are approximate. They are provided so you may return to the segment of the movie I'm referencing.

Digging Deeper. The suggested age for participating in this Bible study is for anyone who believes he or she is old enough to watch the *Harry Potter* movies. If parents give permission, these learners should be able to understand this Bible study. The "Digging Deeper" sections are for those students who are able to grasp deeper concepts. These sections are included so the older learners will grow as well. These sections are also separated under their own "Digging Deeper" headings so teachers can skip them if they believe these concepts are too deep for their younger learners.

Teaching Others. In Chapter One, ten points are given to help readers prepare to engage *Harry Potter* unto the glory of God. In Chapters 2-6, each heading is written in the form of a question. Then, in the paragraphs that follow, I seek to answer each question in light of *Harry Potter* and Scripture. I have organized this book in this way so you may teach others. To teach your students, simply ask the question at the beginning of each section in order to encourage discussion, then read the paragraphs I provide, along with the Scripture references from your Bible.

Each chapter corresponding to the final four *Harry Potter* movies is meant to provide at least 30 minutes of teaching material apart from the "Digging Deeper" sections. Since each *Harry Potter* movie is around 2 hours and 30 minutes in length, there needs to be at least three hours planned per meeting (if the entire movie will be watched in one sitting). If meaningful discussion takes place, these teaching times may be easily expanded into more than an hour of study time together.

In Family Worship. You can use this Bible study to turn family movie night into a family worship time. Many children already participate in the *Harry Potter* series. This study will help transform the way your children participate in all forms of media. Moreover, if they take the Biblical principles learned in this study and apply them to everything in their lives, they will dissect all ideas presented in their cultures based on Scripture, not just media. They will dissect what they're taught in school, what their friends say, what politicians say, what local laws say, etc.

In Neighborhood Outreach. Although it is difficult to reach out to our neighborhoods, this Bible study may help. For example, you can invite your neighborhood over to your own home for a specific night on the weekend for successive weeks to watch the *Harry Potter* movie series and to participate in this Bible study. You can offer popcorn, soda pop, etc. as you engage *Harry Potter* unto the glory of God. Moreover, the gospel is presented numerous times in this Bible study. All hearers will be confronted with the good news of Christ's finished work saving sinners from Satan, God's wrath, and themselves. What a wonderful opportunity to present the gospel!

In a Youth Group or College Age Bible Study. Although this Bible study is intended for anyone capable of understanding *Harry Potter*, it is ideal for teenagers and college students. In order to teach these age groups, you could announce that a Bible study will be taking place at a church member's home on a certain day of the week for a period of 6-weeks during the summer. If the children are still in high school or below, you of course, will need to secure their parents' permission, or you could encourage the parents to attend as well. You could thus come alongside parents in teaching their children to engage media unto God's glory. Unfortunately, many parents merely check the secular rating of media to determine if their children should participate. This method of discernment is a problem because moral media will receive a "safe for children" rating even when it is anti-Christian.

In Personal Bible Study. If you're hoping to be a more discerning Christian, you could use this Bible study to help train yourself to better glorify God as you interact with all media. Also, a necessary by-product is training yourself to glorify God as you interact with all of God's fallen image-bearers, even beyond media.

As Sermon Illustrations. Since each chapter in this Bible study seeks to answer various questions raised by the final four *Harry Potter* movies, you can use them as sermon illustrations. For example, if your sermon seeks to answer the same question I ask, you can follow the timestamp to the example in the *Harry Potter* movie, show the clip, and then use the argumentation and Scripture references I've provided to make your point. These sermon illustrations will serve well to illustrate Scriptural truth, especially to teenage and college age students.

This Bible Study is Based On Three Basic Principles:

First, Participating in Media is an Act of Worship.

Besides the theologians we have in Scripture, there has not been another theologian as influential in the church as early church father Bishop Augustine of Hippo. Although he wrote extensively, his most important writings were against the Pelagians. This group was named after their main leader Pelagius. He was a British monk known for his piety and strict discipline and was later condemned as a heretic.[1]

Augustine taught all humans born since the Fall possessed sinful natures (original sin) from birth (Gen. 3).[2] Pelagius, on the other hand, believed all humans were born as innocent beings who later developed a sinful nature by freely choosing sin from the example of other sinful human beings.[3] In other words, Augustine believed the world is evil because humans are evil, while Pelagius believed humans are evil because the world is evil.

Often in ministry I have observed evangelicals who claim to believe all humans are born sinners (Augustine), and yet live as if their children will be corrupted by outside influences (Pelagius). Parents may profess their children are sinners, but they seek to protect them from a sinful world as if the world is the problem. The problem with our children is not outside influences but is instead their inside influences (Matt. 15:10-11, 17-20). If you and I merely protect our children from external sinful influences, which is impossible in an evil world, we will not address the source of their sin: themselves. Our children are what is wrong with the world; the world is not what is wrong with our children.

Instead of living as if our children "will be" corrupted by the world, we should teach them to handle their own sinful natures in a wicked world. In order to communicate this reality, we must tell our children they are what is wrong with the world. We must teach them they are sinners (Rom. 3:23) in desperate need of a Savior (John 14:6). Apart from His life, death, burial, and resurrection in their stead, there is no hope for them (Rom. 6:23). Christ's finished work is their only hope for being reconciled to God the Father (Rom. 10:9-11; Col. 1:19-22).

By the time our children are 18 years of age, they should be prepared to live in a wicked world in which they are part of the wickedness. Though some may be saved, they must be prepared to face temptation since they still live in an evil world. We must thoroughly teach them the Scriptures and how to recognize the difference between truth and lies in their surrounding culture. If we believe the world is the problem, we will try to shield them from the world; however, if we believe they are the problem, we will instead teach them how to hide the Word of God in their hearts so they might not sin against God (Ps. 119:11).

Because we cannot separate our children from their sinful natures (Augustine), we must prepare them to handle their sinful natures. We must cultivate the fruit of the Spirit in our children, realizing they will always desire wickedness on earth; yet, they must learn to appropriate and cultivate the self-control of God the Holy Spirit, His fruit in their lives (Gal. 5:22-25). One of the biggest problems of children raised by evangelical Christians is they are not prepared to live in this world. Unfortunately, Augustinian parents are practicing the methodology of Pelagians. Our children do not know how to handle temptation whenever they cannot escape it because we have falsely deified our ability to protect our children, thus hindering the cultivation of personal self-control in their lives.

In other words, while trying to protect our children through legalistic boundaries, we have not prepared them to live in this wicked world. Yet temptation will knock on the door unannounced and uninvited (at times welcomed with open arms), and no amount of legalistic boundaries can stop it. If we have not taught our children how to respond to temptation by teaching them how to discern, we doom them for eventual failure.

One way to help our children cultivate discernment in this wicked world is to engage in the media wars with them as a guide. Just as Paul told the Corinthians, "Be imitators of me, as I am of Christ" (1 Cor. 11:1), we too must say to all of our observers, "Be imitators of my media participation, as I am of Christ." Allow me to clarify my suggestion to purposely put ungodly behavior in front of your children. I'm not suggesting you expose children to immorality so that they will know what is immoral. We do not want to tempt our children to sin. Rather, I am suggesting parents thoroughly teach children the Scriptures, and then teach them the difference between truth and lies in pop culture, in light of the Scriptures.

All forms of media, regardless of their rating, intended audience, genre, etc., contain truth and lies woven together into an ungodly web. We must teach our children how to untangle this web. One way to teach our children how to separate truth from lies is to show them how to use discernment as they participate in media. In our media-driven world, our children *will* participate in media, and they will either participate like Christians or like non-Christians. Unfortunately, many evangelical Christians participate in media like non-Christians, simply drinking deeply of all they see and hear without separating truth from lies.

The purpose of this Bible study is to teach Christians how to participate in media unto the glory of God. In order to enjoy God through media, Christians must submit to God's revealed Word in light of Christ's finished work and take every thought captive to obey Christ (2 Cor. 10:5). In other words, I hope to show Christians how to be on their knees in their cultures worshiping God through recognizing His fingerprints in the media produced by God's fallen image-bearers. In the words of Augustine, Christians must plunder the Egyptians:

> For, as the Egyptians had not only the idols and heavy burdens which the people of Israel hated and fled from, but also vessels and ornaments of gold and silver, and garments, which the same people when going out of Egypt appropriated to themselves, designing them for a better use, not doing this on their own authority, but by the

> command of God, the Egyptians themselves, in their ignorance, providing them with things which they themselves, were not making a good use of [Exod. 3:21-22; Exod. 12:35-36]; **in the same way all branches of heathen learning have not only false and superstitious fancies and heavy burdens of unnecessary toil, which every one of us, when going out under the leadership of Christ from the fellowship of the heathen, ought to abhor and avoid; but they contain also liberal instruction which is better adapted to the use of the truth, and some most excellent precepts of morality; and some truths in regard even to the worship of the One God are found among them. Now these are, so to speak, their gold and silver, which they did not create themselves, but dug out of the mines of God's providence which are everywhere scattered abroad, and are perversely and unlawfully prostituting to the worship of devils. These, therefore, the Christian, when he separates himself in spirit from the miserable fellowship of these men, ought to take away from them, and to devote to their proper use in preaching the gospel. Their garments, also,—that is, human institutions such as are adapted to that intercourse with men which is indispensable in this life,—we must take and turn to a Christian use.**[4]

Evangelical Christians must train themselves and their children to plunder pagan media for the "gold" and "silver" and put them to Christian use.

Second, God Owns Everything in His World.

J.K. Rowling (author of *Harry Potter*) and David Yates (director of the final four *Harry Potter* movies) live in the Judeo-Christian God's world. Whether they profess to know Christ or not, all humans live in God's world (Gen. 1:1; Col. 1:16-17). No man can escape this reality.

Furthermore, God created all mankind in His own image to mirror Him in His creation (Gen. 1:26). Notice God created Adam and Eve, telling them, "Be fruitful and multiply and fill the earth and subdue it and have dominion over the fish of the sea and over the birds of the heavens and over every living thing that moves on the earth" (Gen. 1:28). Not only was man meant to mirror God through subduing and exercising dominion over the earth, he was also expected to spread this image of God throughout the earth by having children. Unfortunately, God's image was marred in the Fall of man into sin, but it is still present in humanity, nonetheless. Thus, J.K. Rowling, David Yates, and you and I were created in God's image. So, what does being created in God's image mean?

Theologians hotly debate the implications of mankind as image-bearers suggests, but I believe it includes various elements that separate us from animals: we are spiritual, personal, moral, relational, rational, emotional, and creative beings. Therefore, as Christians recognize these elements of God's image still present in sinful humanity, they can enjoy the God who has gifted these humans. Their giftedness should send Christian observers running to God in worship. Moreover, since Christ is included in the identity of Yahweh as Creator and Sustainer of creation, all creation serves to send observers to Christ in worship as well (Isaiah 42:5; Col. 1:16-17).[5] Thus, for the purpose of recognizing God's image in other humans, let us briefly examine the aforementioned elements that make up His image in humanity.

Man is Spiritual. God is Spirit, and prior to the incarnation, all Persons of the Trinity were Spirit (John 4:24; John 1:1). Since Humans are created in His image, they are spiritual beings as well. Although God spoke the rest of creation into being, He set Adam apart by forming him from the dust of the ground and breathing the breath of life into his nostrils (Gen. 2:7). As a result, humans have eternal souls. At the very least, Rowling argues in *Harry Potter* there is a world beyond the natural world, even arguing that several characters have souls. She is correct. There is a spiritual realm, and the Bible agrees.

Man is Personal. God is personal, distinct. Each Person of the Trinity is distinct from the Other although They are One in essence, and thus, they are one God. Humans are personal beings as well. Each human being is gifted distinctly in life where he or she exists to fulfill his or her cultural purpose unto the glory of God. Rowling is an excellent writer. She vividly creates another world out of thin air in *Harry Potter*. Yates is an excellent director. These movies are well-organized to vividly and visually recreate Rowling's world. Furthermore, in *Harry Potter*, Hermione is an excellent wizard, Ron is great at chess, Harry is a quick learner, etc. All humans, though similar, are distinctly different; and the main characters in *Harry Potter* agree.

Man is Relational. God has always been relational in the Trinity. There is one God who exists in three Persons. These Three have loved and enjoyed one another from eternity past (Gen. 1:1; John 1:1; Rom. 8:9). Man, due to reflecting God, desires relationship as well. When Adam was in the Garden naming every animal the Bible argues clearly there was not a helper fit for him (Gen. 2:20). God says, "It is not good that the man should be alone; I will make him a helper fit for him" (Gen. 2:18). Marriage proves man is relational. Moreover, man's relational nature is proven by God's creation of families, nations, neighbors, friendship, the church, etc. and man's enjoyment of these various avenues of relationship.

Man is Rational. God is rational. The laws of logic flow from His identity, governing all communication within the Trinity and creation.[6] Moreover, the fact God gave humans brains and the ability to communicate and function in this world proves man is rational. Apart from being rational, you couldn't read these words, turn these pages, etc. Furthermore, if you tried to communicate with your family and friends, if humans aren't rational beings, they could never understand you. God gave humans His written Word because humans are rational beings (2 Tim. 3:16-17).

Man is Emotional. God has emotions which are displayed throughout Scripture (Num. 12:9; 2 Kings 22:13; Josh. 24:19; Ps. 145:8; 2 Pet. 3:9; etc.). These emotions, however, are neither human nor marred by sin. God is holy and perfectly emotional without compromising His other attributes. Man was created in God's image to mirror God's emotional nature.[7] Man's emotions, however, are distinctly human and are marred by sin. Emotions are expressed throughout the *Harry Potter* series: anger, sorrow, joy, hate, etc.

Man is Creative. God is obviously creative. Look around you at the wonderful creation God designed and spoke into being (Gen. 1-2)! As humans mirror, or reflect, God they have an innate desire to create, as well. All artistry, media, vocations, clothes, hair styles, etc. contain fingerprints of the creating work of humans. Rowling's and Yates's creative fingerprints are all over the *Harry Potter* series: they created a fantasy world, supernatural entities, magic, spells, humor, special effects, etc. Through this creativity, since God is mirrored, Christians can enjoy God.

Man is Moral. God is holy (Ps. 99:9). He is morally perfect. Humans are capable of living moral lives. God has supplied all humans with consciences which are moral compasses that help them discern basic morality (Rom. 2:14-15; John 1:4). Sin, of course, keeps us from living morally perfect lives (Rom. 3); however, humans are still capable of thinking and doing "good" things. Unfortunately, we still miss the mark with our good deeds and fail to perfectly please God (Rom. 3:23), but humanity is obviously not as evil as it could be. Moreover, morality is displayed throughout the *Harry Potter* series. There is a clear good (Harry Potter), and a clear evil (Lord Voldermort).

Third, Man Was Created To Always Be Dependent On God's Word.

Finally, even though man was created in God's image, he was never meant to be a little god, or, as Satan put it, "like God" (Gen. 3:5). Even in the Garden of Eden man was created to be ever dependent on God and His Word (Gen. 1-3). God even conversed and fellowshiped with man in the Garden. Humans were meant to enjoy God forever in a wonderful, sinless world but man sinned.

Since the Fall of man into sin, humans need God's Word even more due to the darkness of sin permeating all creation (Gen. 3). Thus, as Christians interact with culture, they must put on "God's Truth" glasses by comparing and contrasting all they see with the Word of God. All forms of media either reveal God's glory by agreeing with God's Word or hide God's glory by telling lies. All forms of media make truth claims, whether they claim to be fiction or non-fiction. The authors, characters, directors, etc. are always arguing a point, perspective or truth-claim, and their arguments either agree or disagree with God's Word. Christians must test all things, keeping what is true, trashing what is false, while constantly revealing where these authors of media admit they live in our God's world.

In God's world, all truth is God's truth and all lies are the devil's lies. In other words, Christians know the "Why" behind the truth presented by God's image-bearers. We know our Creator intimately through Scripture and through Jesus Christ. The world knows our Creator as well, but they often suppress this truth (Rom. 1). Because all humans possess some knowledge of our God, Christians must participate in media and in the rest of the world for the purpose of recognizing where the world admits they live in our God's world. As we recognize this reality, we will be on our knees in our cultures in worship to the Triune God who gave His only Son to redeem sinners and sinful creation (Rom. 8:19-23).

---

[1] Justo L. González, *The Story of Christianity: The Early Church to the Dawn of the Reformation* (San Francisco: Harper & Row, 1984), 214.
[2] Ibid., 214-215.
[3] Ibid., 215.
[4] Marcus Dods, ed., *The Works of Aurelius Augustine, Bishop of Hippo: A New Translation, Vol. IX – On Christian Doctrine; The Enchiridion; On Catechising; and On Faith and the Creed* (Edinburgh: T. & T. Clark, 1892), 76.
[5] Richard Bauckham, *Jesus and the God of Israel: God Crucified and Other Studies on the New Testament's Christology of Divine Identity* (Grand Rapids: Eerdmans, 2008), 27-28.

[6] John Frame, "Presuppositional Apologetics," In *Five Views on Apologetics*, ed. Stanley N. Gundry and Steven B. Cowan (Grand Rapids: Zondervan, 2000), 225-226.
[7] Bruce A. Ware, *God's Greater Glory: The Exalted God of Scripture and the Christian Faith* (Wheaton, Ill: Crossway Books, 2004), 146.

1
HOW TO ENJOY GOD THROUGH HARRY POTTER

Depending on who you talk with in the evangelical community, you'll receive a variety of opinions concerning *Harry Potter*: "Christians shouldn't watch it;" "Christians can enjoy God through it;" and even, "It's of the devil!" As already revealed in the title of this chapter and the title of this book, I believe *Harry Potter*, although it contains evil things, is still an avenue through which Christians can enjoy God. Many characters involved in the story and all the humans involved in creating the *Harry Potter* series subtly admit to living in our God's world. As a result, it is possible to enjoy God through *Harry Potter*, but there are certain steps we must take.

In order to enjoy God through *Harry Potter* we must...

1) Know what the Bible explicitly says.

The various commands found in Scripture concerning what is good and what is evil must be committed to our memories. With Christ as the theme of Scripture, we must have the Word of God hidden in our hearts for the purpose of not sinning against God (Ps. 119:11). It is *impossible* to be discerning as a Christian if we do *not* know what the Scriptures teach. Untruth is only recognized whenever it is compared with truth.

2) Know what the Bible implicitly says.

The various commands, narratives, etc. in the Scriptures *imply* truth as well. Understanding the natural outworking of theology is dreadfully lacking in Christianity. For example, if this world belongs to God, then all truth whether public or private belongs to *Him*. Thus, there is no such thing as a neutral approach to anything in God's world. Everything is either likeminded with God or is anti-God. Therefore, every movie, TV show, song, book, etc. argues from a specific view of the world which is likeminded with God or is anti-God or, most likely, is a combination of both. This is why Christians must test all things.

Furthermore, since Christ claims to be the Way, the Truth, and the Life, the only Way to God the Father, all truth must be rightly understood in light of His incarnation, life, death, and resurrection (John 14:6). So when media speaks about God, the test concerning who they are *really* speaking about is their view of His Son Jesus Christ. If they reject Jesus as the Only Way of Salvation, God the Son, the Way, the Truth, and the Life, then they are anti-God regardless if they agree with the rest of the Bible (John 5:17-47).

3) Think about the surface ideas being presented.

Think about everything you are seeing and hearing. What is the point? What are the characters trying or hoping to accomplish? What do they reveal about their view of the world? Do they openly admit they live in our God's world? What must you do to destroy arguments and every lofty opinion raised against the knowledge of God, in order to take these obvious ideas captive to obey Christ (2 Cor. 10:5)?

4) Think about the underlying ideas being presented.

This step goes beyond the characters and asks questions concerning the author. What is the agenda of the author? Why has he or she included the various characters, plots, subplots, themes, etc.? What is his or her point? These worldview implications may be more subtle and harder to recognize.

5) Compare and contrast all ideas with Scripture.

Does the idea that the media is presenting line up with Scripture? Is it true, or must we *correct* it with Scriptural truth? What must we trash? What can we keep? Which truths reveal the author lives in our God's world? What truths must we pluck from *Harry Potter* and connect to God through Christ in light of Scripture?

6) Understand the author beyond what she is presenting.

Some ideas are very subtle, so subtle, in fact, that apart from possessing an accurate understanding of the author, the true meaning will escape us. Is there anything presented in *Harry Potter* which spurs us to examine the author's beliefs beyond what she has written so we can have a greater understanding of the foundation from which she is arguing?

7) Possess a Christ-centered understanding of Scripture.

If we don't see Jesus as the theme of Scripture, then we are tempted to view movies that merely emphasize Biblical morality as "Christian," and think God has been glorified. The problem is the Bible is not mainly a book about morals, but, rather, it is a book about Jesus. The movie, *The Book of Eli*, for example, teaches the Bible is a moral guideline which humanity can accomplish perfectly. Jesus is not mentioned one time the entire movie, so it may be a fallacy to call it a "Christian" movie.

Since Christ is the theme of the Bible, it is *impossible* to be Biblical without understanding what Christ has accomplished in the place of sinners through His life, death, and resurrection. For this reason, it is very important *Harry Potter* is not merely compared and contrasted with the Scriptures morally, but is also compared and contrasted with Christ being the remedy for all the evil that exists in the world, the Answer for the sin problem. *Harry Potter* seeks to provide an answer for the sin problem. You must compare Rowling's answer with God's answer found in Scripture.

8) Keep our minds working throughout the *Harry Potter* movie(s).

If we are not intentional, we will daydream or lose focus while processing *nothing* through our "Christian filters" as we take in media. Not thinking is directly forbidden in Scripture (Phil. 4:8). The problem with not thinking on truth is we are commanded to take every thought captive to obey Christ (2 Cor. 10:5). Thus, everything must be taken in and filtered through God's perfect Word in light of Christ's finished work. Christians then must carry out the command found in Philippians 4:8:

> [8]Finally, brothers, whatever is true, whatever is honorable, whatever is just, whatever is pure,

whatever is lovely, whatever is commendable, if there is any excellence, if there is anything worthy of praise, think about these things.

As we watch *Harry Potter*, here are some good questions to ask of the various ideas being presented in light of Philippians 4:8: 1) Is this true? 2) Is this honorable? 3) Is this just? 4) Is this pure? 5) Is this lovely? 6) Is this commendable? 7) Is this excellent? 8) Is this praise worthy? If the answer is "no" to any of these questions, then the idea being presented must be discarded or corrected in light of Scriptural truth. We must be actively dissecting everything we see and hear, trashing lies while keeping and thinking on truth.

9) Know how Christianity answers man's basic worldview questions.

Nancy Pearcey, *Total Truth* author and tutor at Rivendell Sanctuary, lists three worldview subjects all humanity examines, questions, and answers:

> 1) CREATION: How did it all begin? Where did we come from? 2) FALL: What went wrong? What is the source of evil and suffering? 3) REDEMPTION: What can we do about it? How can the world be set right again?[8]

The Bible argues: 1) CREATION: The only God who exists created all things, including you, for His own glory (Gen. 1; especially Gen. 1:26; Col. 1:16-17). 2) FALL:

Adam and Eve sinned against God, and all creation, including humanity, fell into sin (Gen. 3; Rom. 3:10-23; Rom. 8:20-22). Thus, all humans are sinners which means we are what is wrong with the world (Rom. 3:23; Gal. 3:22). 3) REDEMPTION: God the Son incarnate, Jesus Christ, came to earth to fix what Adam destroyed. Jesus Christ, through His life, death, and resurrection, is the only Answer for the sin problem (Rom. 8:1-39; John 14:6). Almost every movie, TV show, song, or book seeks to answer at least one of the above questions, and many try to answer all of them. The problem is most of these forms of media provide the wrong answers. Discernment, therefore, is *essential* for Christians living in a media world where wickedness and lies are placed side by side and interlaced with truth.

Digging Deeper:
10) **Possess a basic understanding of philosophy.**

The movie, *The Matrix,* is based on a specific philosophical idea that cannot be understood properly by simply watching the movie. Furthermore, *The Matrix* trilogy of movies presents many other philosophical ideas throughout. Christian ideas make their way into these movies, but these ideas are placed directly next to Buddhist and Gnostic ideas. If you understand the Scriptures, you *may* recognize these Buddhist and Gnostic ideas are not true, but if you hope to understand why the author includes these ideas and what specific worldview the author presents, you will need a basic understanding of philosophy.

Summary

To summarize, this Bible study is based on the foundation that Christians should engage their cultures, find the common examples of God's image therein, extract these common truths, and add Scriptural Truth to them: 1) Man is sinful (Rom. 3:23). 2) God's answer for the sin problem is Christ's redeeming work in reconciling sinners and creation to His Father (John 14:6). As you watch *Harry Potter*, ask *at least* these 3 questions: 1) What ideas should I accept because they are in full agreement with Scripture? 2) What must I reject because it is in full disagreement with Scripture? 3) What half-truths, in order to be made completely true, must be extracted from *Harry Potter* and connected to God's Word in light of man's sinful condition and Christ's creating, sustaining, and redeeming work?

A Final Hint

Since these *Harry Potter* movies say nothing about God or Jesus Christ, there is nothing in *Harry Potter* that can be accepted or received by Christians based on its own merit without adding truth. Everything will need to be dissected. As a result, as you watch and hear the various ideas in *Harry Potter* you will only have two choices: 1) Trash what you see and hear, or 2) Qualify what you see and hear with

Scripture to make it obey Christ according to the entire Bible.

---

[8] Nancy Pearcey, *Total Truth: Liberating Christianity from Its Cultural Captivity* (Wheaton, Ill: Crossway Books, 2004), 25.

2

EVIL ELEMENTS PRESENT IN THE HARRY POTTER SERIES

Like most forms of media, there are elements in *Harry Potter* Christians must reject. We must be careful, however, not to throw the baby out with the bathwater. Because *Harry Potter* contains evil elements, some Christians reject *Harry Potter* completely as if the entire series is evil. If a form of media contains *some* evil elements, it does not necessarily mean it is *entirely* evil. Just like the Bible is not entirely evil because it contains examples of evil, *Harry Potter* is not entirely evil because it contains examples of evil.

Christians must be consistent in how they seek to apply Scripture to their daily lives. They cannot merely pick and choose what media Christians may participate in based on some biased, arbitrary opinion. If the Bible is not entirely evil even though it contains some evil elements, then media that also contains some evil elements is not entirely evil either. Therefore, in this section, we will take these absolute evils present in *Harry Potter*, extract them, and discard them. This will leave us with elements that contain both good and evil which we can examine based on the Scriptures.

What Does God Think About Witchcraft and Wizardry?

The *Harry Potter* series is full of witchcraft and wizardry. Although Rowling uses witchcraft and wizardry primarily as a literary device, this does not negate the reality that she makes truth claims concerning good magic vs. bad magic. In other words, magic is not a neutral literary device.

According to Scripture, all witchcraft and wizardry must be trashed, since the practice of divination directly violates God's Word. There is no such thing as *good* magic, sorcery, or witchcraft. All forms of witchcraft and wizardry are evil. Here are just a few Scripture verses for reference:

> Exodus 22:18 – [18]You shall not permit a **sorceress** to live.
>
> Deuteronomy 18:10 – [10]There shall not be found among you anyone who burns his son or his daughter as an offering, **anyone who practices divination or tells fortunes or interprets omens, or a sorcerer**.
>
> Acts 16:16-18 – [16]As we were going to the place of prayer, we were met by a slave girl who had a **spirit**

of divination and brought her owners much gain by **fortune-telling**. ¹⁷She followed Paul and us, crying out, "These men are servants of the Most High God, who proclaim to you the way of salvation." ¹⁸And this she kept doing for many days. Paul, having become greatly annoyed, turned and said to the spirit, "I command you in the name of Jesus Christ to come out of her." And it came out that very hour.

Galatians 5:19-20 – ¹⁹Now the works of the flesh are evident: sexual immorality, impurity, sensuality, ²⁰idolatry, **sorcery**, enmity, strife, jealousy, fits of anger, rivalries.

Practicing sorcery, witchcraft, divination, etc. are all unbiblical attempts to gain special knowledge or power *apart* from God and His revealed Word, the Bible. Since God has not chosen to reveal Himself in this way, the source of knowledge and power through this method is Satan, his demons, or our own flesh. If you receive any knowledge or witness any power through witchcraft or wizardry, the devil is the source. We must ask ourselves if we would rather submit to God or submit to the devil. If we submit to God through Christ, then we must *reject* all forms of sorcery, witchcraft, divination, etc.

What Does God Think About Inappropriate Language?

Scattered sparsely throughout these movies is inappropriate

language. Inappropriate language is commonly understood based on the culture in which you live. If a specific culture says certain words are vulgar or inappropriate, then these words are vulgar or inappropriate in that culture. For Christians, inappropriate language extends beyond mere vulgarity to whatever words are not edifying or encouraging (Eph. 4:29). There are several instances in these movies where friends hurt one another, students tear one another down, etc.

Have you ever hurt one of your friends or family members with your words? There is nothing wrong with joking with friends; however, when we hurt one another with our words, we sin against God. As Christians, in whatever we do, whether in word or deed, we must do everything in the name of the Lord Jesus, giving thanks to God the Father through Him (Col. 3:17).

Moreover, God's name is used in vain several times in this movie series. God's name is to be revered. He is the Creator and Sustainer of all things (Gen. 1:1; Col. 1:16-17). The only reason you and I have tongues and brains capable of speech is because God has given us these gifts and sustains them. Christians must reject all unedifying and blaspheming language. Here are some helpful Scripture references:

> James 1:26 – [26]If anyone thinks he is religious and does not bridle his tongue but deceives his heart, this person's religion is worthless.

James 3:5-6 – ⁵So also the tongue is a small member, yet it boasts of great things. How great a forest is set ablaze by such a small fire! ⁶And the tongue is a fire, a world of unrighteousness. The tongue is set among our members, staining the whole body, setting on fire the entire course of life, and set on fire by hell.

Ephesians 4:29 – ²⁹Let no corrupting talk come out of your mouths, but only such as is good for building up, as fits the occasion, that it may give grace to those who hear.

Exodus 20:7 – ⁷You shall not take the name of the LORD your God in vain, for the LORD will not hold him guiltless who takes his name in vain.

As pilgrims in this evil world, Christians should seek to build up one another in holiness toward God as a result of believing Christ is the only Way to be brought into right relationship with God, that He is the only Way of salvation from sin and its penalty (John 14:6; Eph. 4:29). Our speech to and about one another should be seasoned with grace. Furthermore, we should always speak God's name with awe and reverence since we know Him in a greater way than the rest of the world due to Scripture and Christ (2 Tim. 3:16-17; Rom. 1; Col. 2:2-3; John 1:1).

What Does God Think About Revenge?

Revenge plays a central role in the themes of the *Harry*

Potter series. Harry wants to kill Lord Voldermort for hurting his family and his friends. Christians, on the other hand, should seek justice, *not* revenge. According to God's standard, man achieves justice either righteously or unrighteously leaving no room for mere revenge. Revenge or "vigilante justice" is *unrighteous*. Christians must make sure they do not desire revenge in their daily lives.

Whenever we watch the nightly news, watch a movie, or read a book; and we see a man or woman hunted down by his or her victim, a rogue cop, a family member, etc., we must remind ourselves that vengeance is ultimately the Lord's (Rom. 12:19); but while humanity is on earth, He has given this charge to His ministers, the government (Rom. 13:1-7). When they fail, Christians should trust the Lord's coming vengeance instead of seeking their own (Rom. 12:19). On the other side, whenever the government fulfills its role as God's ministers of justice on earth, we can enjoy the Lord through their picture of His justice. When Christians are tempted by fictional media and the nightly news to seek their own form of justice, we must run to the truth of God's Word, trusting Him beyond our own wicked desire to say, "Vengeance is mine, I will repay, says sovereign me!" Thus, we must reject Harry's desire for revenge in this series. Exactly how we must reject his desire for revenge will be revealed later in this study.

Digging Deeper:
What Does God Think About Dualism?

Dualism is the belief that there are two opposing, eternal, *equal* forces in the universe known as good and evil. This lie is prevalent in most forms of media. The *Harry Potter* series gives the impression that evil may defeat good.

Throughout this series, the "chosen one," Harry Potter, represents good while Lord Voldermort represents evil. In Scripture, there's never any question if God will bring about what He says He will. There's not a question concerning Who has won, is winning, and will win.

Granted, in our daily lives, as we live in an evil world, it may *appear* good and evil are equal, but we have the assurance of Scripture and Christ's resurrection, that even death is overcome by God through Christ (Mark 16:6). Every evil, all the results of sin, have been conquered by Christ: Satan, sickness, death, pain, disease, famine, storms, etc. This reality will be fully realized when Christians live forevermore in the new heavens and the new earth (Rev. 21).

Furthermore, even Satan is given life from God (Col. 1:16-17). He can do nothing apart from God's allowance. We see this mystery throughout Scripture: 1) In Job 1 and 2 God gives Satan permission to attack Job. 2) In Acts 2:23, Peter preaches at Pentecost telling his audience, "[23]This Jesus, delivered up according to the definite plan and foreknowledge of God, you crucified and killed by the hands of lawless men." We also learn in Luke 22:3 Satan entered Judas and betrayed Christ. 3) In 2 Corinthians 12, the apostle Paul speaks about a "thorn in the flesh" he prayed for God to remove, yet he calls it a "messenger of Satan" God used to teach him His grace was sufficient. The point is simply that both good and evil fit into the plan of God without making God evil. He is infinitely greater than evil. The history of creation and redemption as revealed in Scripture prove God is infinitely greater than evil. The Triune God existed prior to evil, and He will continue existing after the judgment of evil fully comes to pass.

3

HARRY POTTER AND THE ORDER OF THE PHOENIX

[After watching *Harry Potter and the Order of the Phoenix*]

Are We Willing to Lay Down Our Lives for Our Enemies?

At the beginning of the movie, even though Dudley says some very nasty things about Harry, his deceased friend, and his mom, Harry still saves Dudley from the dementors. Harry risked his life for Dudley. Would you have done the same?

In light of Christ's command, Christians should indeed "love their enemies, and pray for those who persecute them" (Matt. 5:43-44). Harry was willing to sacrifice his own life for the sake of his mean cousin, his enemy. Christians today, likewise, should do the same for their enemies. Why would Christ command Christians to love their enemies? The answer is found in looking at what Christ did for His enemies (sinners).

God has proven His love for sinners by sending His one and only Son to die for them (John 3:16; Rom. 5:8). Thus, God offers sinners eternal life where they can enjoy Him forevermore (Rom. 6:23). The only Way for a sinner to be brought into right relationship with God is through Christ (John 14:6). Even though we were God's enemies due to our rebellion, Christ still died for us (Rom. 8:1-11). Even when the Roman soldiers nailed Him to the cross, Jesus said, "Father, forgive them, for they know not what they do" (Luke 23:34). As a result of Christ's finished work, all those who come to God through Christ are called to love their enemies as well (Matt. 5:43-48). As Christians look to Christ alone for their salvation, they must love as He loved and live as He lived. Jesus laid down His life for His enemies. Are we willing to do the same? If we have been transformed by Christ, we must love our enemies like Christ did (1 Pet. 2:20-25). One of the nuggets of truth found in *Harry Potter* is a self-sacrificial act done in the same manner as Christ. Therefore, Christians are right to value this behavior since it mimics their Savior.

Should Christians Stand Up for Truth?

At about 00:22:00, Dumbledore begins defending Harry before the Ministry of Magic, because Harry used magic in front of a muggle. He defends Harry based on truth.

Furthermore, at around 00:35:30, Harry stands up for the truth that Lord Voldermort is back from the "dead." Harry was willing to proclaim truth that was unpopular, truth that was viewed as a lie by those in power. Does this sound familiar?

Today, many of those in pop culture, the media, and in academia, as well, refer to Christ's death, burial, and resurrection, along with the Scriptures, as myths or lies. Like Harry, Christians, too, must stand up unashamedly and proclaim truth in a world that denies the truth. Christians must always be ready to give a defense with gentleness and respect to anyone who asks for a reason for the hope that is in them (1 Pet. 3:15).

Regardless of the opposition, for the sake of defeating evil and loving his neighbor, Harry forms and trains an army for eventually battling Lord Voldermort. If Harry listened to those who denied this truth, he would not be prepared to face the evil one when the time came. Harry chose to live in response to truth instead of merely following the opinions of the powerful.

Likewise, if Christians listen to the world, we will not be prepared to face the evil one on a daily basis. We must be willing to stand up, learn truth, and live in response to it. In our world, everyone wants to do what they want until their "freedoms" are "violated." Post-moderns cling to the idea of relative truth—that objective truth does not exist and values are personal and subjective, not universal and objective—until terrorists fly two planes into the Twin Towers. Then, the reality of evil comes crashing down and we find ourselves easily making truth claims: Terrorism is evil. Evil exists, and humanity screams out for a hero; however, his name is not Harry Potter. His name is Jesus Christ.

Are All Humans Equally Valuable?

Throughout this movie Harry emphasizes the value of Cedric, the human being Lord Voldermort murdered. Christians, likewise, must place a high value on human life. The Bible clearly separates humans apart from all other creation on earth by arguing God created humanity in His own image (Gen. 1:26). All humans are valuable, regardless of their age or location, or what other humans may believe. The value of humanity comes from God alone, not the mere opinions of men. Thus, Christians should value all humans the same whether they're in the womb, the hospital, nursing home, etc. Do you value all humans the same regardless of their age or location?

Can We Really Do or Be Anything We Want, If We Just Put Our Minds to It?

At around 00:59:50, when Harry is training the other students to be part of the army against Lord Voldermort, Harry says,

> Working hard is important, but there's something that matters even more: believing in yourself. Think of it this way; every great wizard in history started out as nothing more than what we are now, students. If they can do it, why not us?

Is this true? Can every human being be or do whatever his heart desires? No.

Humans can only rise to the point their God-given natural abilities will allow them. All the gifts you and I possess were given to us in the womb. Some humans are good at math, others are good at English; some students are good with their hands, while others have great ability to understand difficult academic subjects. Whoever you are, be who God created you to be. Take your natural abilities to their consistent (logical) end unto the glory of God.

If the above is true, and it is also true that all humans were "fearfully" and "wonderfully" made by God in the womb (Ps. 139:14), then everything we do must be done unto the glory of God (1 Cor. 10:31). He is the source of life; therefore, all life exists for His glory (Col. 1:16-17). As a result, Christians should seek to be distinctly Christian in all they do.

Moreover, there are no insignificant vocations in God's world. Everything either reveals God's glory or hides it. Christian, as you come to God through Christ, make sure you carry out your daily duties, whether working or playing, eating or drinking, in such a way that you reveal this undeniable reality: all humans live in God's world, and He is worthy of our worship, worthy of being enjoyed through His provisions.

Does Satan Rest?

At around 01:06:00, we see Professor Snape training Harry to keep Lord Voldermort from penetrating his mind. Harry says, "Stop it." Professor Snape responds, "Is this what you call control?" Harry exclaims, "We've been at it for hours. If we could just rest?" Snape answers, "The Dark Lord isn't resting." Satan is similar to Lord Voldermort in that he doesn't rest either. Ever since Genesis 3, Satan is found lurking behind virtually all evil acts and thoughts present in the Scriptures. He is even prowling around today like a roaring lion looking for people to devour. Thus, Christians must always be sober-minded and watchful for the activity of the evil one (1 Pet. 5:8). Just when life seems to be going well and there is the appearance of peace, Satan, directly or indirectly, rears his ugly head.

Do Only Your Outward Actions Determine If You are Good or Bad?

At around 01:11:00, Harry says,

> This connection between me and Voldermort, what if the reason for it is that I am becoming more like him? I just feel so angry all the time, and what if after everything that I've been through, something's gone wrong inside me? What if I'm becoming bad?

Sirius responds,

> I want you to listen to me very carefully Harry. You're not a bad person. You are a very good person who bad things have happened to. You understand? Besides, the world isn't split into good people and Death Eaters. We've all got both light and dark inside of us. What matters is the part we choose to act on. That's who we really are.

Is Sirius right? Do the decisions we make, the part inside of us we choose to act on, either light or dark, make us who we *really* are? No.

The Bible argues all humans since Adam are sinners (Rom. 3:23) (except for Christ - Heb. 4:15). We can indeed choose whether or not we will be moral today, but we cannot choose to be sinless since it is indeed part of our heart, our identity (Gal. 3:22; 1 John 1:8-10). To borrow from Sirius's statement, we indeed have both light (God's image) and dark (sinful nature) within us; the difference is that the mere existence of the dark (sinful nature) within us condemns us before God the Father. Thus, even if you do your best to act on the good within you, you still cannot reverse or remedy the wages of any amount of sin: death (Rom. 3:23). You need someone who is sinless to come, take your place, to die for your sins, and reconcile you to God. On the cross Jesus died as if He committed your sins and mine so that those who come to God through Him can be treated as if they lived the perfect righteous life He lived (2 Cor. 5:20-21).

Furthermore, this Individual we need to save us, Jesus Christ, cannot be only a man, for He must also be able to forgive our sins. The forgiving of sins is something only God can do (Mark 2:5-12). God must save, and He has done this very thing in Christ Jesus, God the Son (John 1:1-3). Have you come to God the Father through God the Son (John 14:6)?

Did Jesus Take Responsibility for Sins He Did Not Commit?

At around 01:20:30, Dumbledore takes responsibility for Harry disobeying the Ministry of Magic. Did Dumbledore actually order Harry to prepare this army? No. Likewise, even though Jesus never sinned, He took responsibility for our sins, even to the point of dying for them (Isaiah 53:4-6). Dumbledore took responsibility for Harry's breaking of the law, but then fled from punishment. Jesus, on the other hand, willfully accepted the punishment and laid down His life for sinners by drinking the cup of His Father's wrath (Matt. 26:36-44; John 10:14-18). This reality is a great mystery. Nevertheless, let us believe what the Scripture says: "My Father, if it be possible, let this cup pass from me; nevertheless, not as I will, but as you will" (Matt. 26:39). Jesus dreaded being punished by His Father for the sins of humanity, yet He willfully satisfied (propitiated) His

Father's wrath toward sinners through His suffering and death (1 John 2:2, 4:10), so that those who come to God through Him would be shown one hundred percent mercy and forgiveness. Why do people reject such wonderful grace?

Can God Be Enjoyed Through Experiencing the Love of Friends and Family?

Near the end of the movie Lord Voldermort attacks Harry internally. As Harry lies on the ground in pain, Dumbledore says to him, "Harry, it isn't how you are alike, it's how you are not." As he continues to writhe in pain, Harry's friends come into the room, which reminds him of all the love he's experienced in his life through friends and family. Harry then says to Lord Voldermort, "You're the weak one, and you'll never know love or friendship, and I feel sorry for you." Lord Voldermort then leaves Harry's body and tells him, "You're a fool Harry Potter, and you will lose everything." Who is correct in this exchange, Lord Voldermort or Harry Potter? Harry Potter, of course!

God has indeed provided love and friendship so that humanity would enjoy these things. We, however, must be careful not to assume these things should be enjoyed based on their own worth or merit *apart* from God. On the contrary, God has given humanity love and friendship for the purpose of enjoying *God* through enjoying love and friendship with those around us. Also, since Christ is revealed as Creator with Yahweh, He is the Creator of love and friendship; therefore, love and friendship cannot be understood apart from a Scriptural understanding of Christ (John 1:1-3; Col. 1:16-17). In other words, since Christians know God through Christ, only we experience love and friendship the way God intended.

Is God In Control of All Things?

At the end of the movie, Dumbledore shares why he had been avoiding Harry. Harry lacked understanding concerning why Dumbledore wouldn't listen to him. He thought Dumbledore might be angry with Him. As a result, Harry was sad and confused. Dumbledore, however, had Harry's best interests in mind.

In similar manner, just as Dumbledore was avoiding Harry for his benefit, God does things we don't understand at times for the sake of our benefit, as well (Rom. 8:28). The apostle Paul had a "thorn in the flesh" he prayed for God to remove three times, but God didn't remove it (2 Cor. 12:2-10). Why? Paul answers that God didn't remove this thorn because He was teaching Paul that His grace was sufficient even in the midst of him suffering with a "thorn in the flesh."

We may be tempted to believe God should remove all effects of the Fall from our lives: disease, storms, oppressors, famine, droughts, etc. But only God, in His sovereignty, may choose to allow such things in our lives.

Only God knows what is best for us, since He is all knowing. He is, indeed, working all things together for good, for those who love Him, those who are called according to His purpose (Rom. 8:28). At the end of the day, as we sometimes suffer in this evil world, we may still enjoy God because, even in our suffering, He is working all things out for good!

Digging Deeper:
Should Christians Turn the Other Cheek?

At the beginning of the movie, after Harry questions Dudley about beating up a 10 year old, Dudley and his friends make fun of Harry by saying mean things about him, his deceased friend Cedric, and his parents. Harry escalates the situation by threatening Dudley with magic and putting his wand to Dudley's chin. Based on the Scriptures, did Harry obey God in his response to being bullied? No.

Jesus teaches us how Christians should respond to persecution in Matthew 5:38-42:

> [38] You have heard that it was said, 'An eye for an eye and a tooth for a tooth.' [39] But I say to you, Do not resist the one who is evil. But if anyone slaps you on the right cheek, turn to him the other also. [40] And if anyone would sue you and take your tunic, let him have your cloak as well. [41] And if anyone forces you to go one mile, go with him two

miles. ⁴²Give to the one who begs from you, and do not refuse the one who would borrow from you.

These verses seem to suggest that Christians are never to fight against those who try to hurt them, but what about the command from Christ to love our neighbors as ourselves (Matt. 22:39)? If loving ourselves according to Christ's words means never protecting our lives, then if we love our neighbors *as ourselves*, one may assume we should never protect *their lives* either.

In September 2011, a former deacon walked into Lakeland Church in Florida, after murdering his own wife, and shot his pastor in the back of the head as he knelt praying. The shooter then fired three bullets into the associate pastor, but was tackled by some other congregants before he could do more damage. Based on the words of Christ above, were these Christians wrong to stop this man from shooting other people? No, because it seems Jesus's point in the Sermon on the Mount is to declare the end of the theocracy in Israel.

Jesus has fulfilled the Law (Matt. 5:17). Christians are no longer under the Law of Israel in a civil sense, but are instead under the civil law of the local government (Rom. 13:1-7). Thus, God's holiness is no longer directly associated with a specific national people on earth. His holiness is, instead, associated with His church through Christ. This church of Christ, however, although existing on earth, is part of a heavenly kingdom that is *not* part of this world (John 18:36). Hence, Jesus's command to "turn the other cheek" must be applied *only* to Christians who are suffering *because* they are members of this heavenly kingdom. In Israel, the reason for the attack had little significance, for the "eye for an eye" law remained. But Jesus says that since His kingdom has come, the reason for the attack has huge significance. Hurting other humans in the civil kingdom may be avenged by the sword (Rom. 13:1-7), but persecution of the heavenly kingdom may not be avenged except by God (Rom. 12:18-21).

God has judged the sins of His people in Christ, thus reconciling them to Himself (2 Cor. 5:18). As a result, Christians too must carry out their ministry of reconciliation with their enemies since they are part of His heavenly kingdom and this heavenly ethic (2 Cor. 5:17-21). Just as Christ suffered for His church, Christians too should arm themselves with the same mind by being willing to suffer for the name of Christ (1 Pet. 4:1-2).

David VanDrunen, Professor of Systematic Theology and Ethics at Westminster Seminary California, communicates this reality well:

> Finally, the legitimacy of self-defense depends upon the context: am I being assailed as just another citizen of the civil kingdom or as a disciple of Jesus and hence as a member of the church? If an individual Christian is threatened by a burglar who breaks into his home to steal his property, this is an ordinary civil matter, and the Christian (who, in

this setting, just happens to be a Christian) is free (and perhaps even obligated?) to defend himself or seek coercive legal remedy. But if an individual Christian is threatened because of her Christian faith, because she is identified with Christ as a member of his church, then is non-retaliation perhaps the appropriate response? The context of Matt 5:38-42 suggests an affirmative answer. Jesus most likely envisions his disciples being slapped, stripped, and conscripted not in ordinary civil disputes but specifically *as his disciples*: "Blessed are those who are persecuted *because of righteousness*, for theirs is the kingdom of heaven. Blessed are you when people insult you, persecute you and falsely say all kinds of evil against you *because of me*" (5:10-11). The apostolic example suggests that Christians, in the face of state action, may peaceably appeal to the civil government to abide by its own laws (e.g., Acts 22:25-29). The apostles, however, never retaliated when government officials treated them unjustly and never pursued legal action against those who persecuted them. The disruption of the civil kingdom may be avenged by the sword but the persecution of the kingdom of heaven may not.[9]

In other words, if a bully persecutes you because you're a Christian, enjoy the fact that even the devil and his servants recognize you're a Christian (Acts 5:41). However, if a bully attacks you for other reasons, you should protect the image of God in you (or others, for that matter) as an act of obedience to Christ (Col. 1:16-17). The attack is not a heavenly kingdom matter (Gen. 1:26) but, rather, one suffered as a result of citizenry in the fallen civil kingdom (Rom. 13:1-7).

Concerning the protection of your family, do not strip them of the privilege of suffering for the sake of Christ if they are Christians and so choose (Luke 6:22). If someone merely wants to snuff out the image of God in them, then protect your wife and children to the point of laying down your life for them (Eph. 5:25). Christians are not to be doormats in the civil kingdom since we are indeed citizens here (Rom. 13:1-7; Col. 1:16-17). However, we are not yet fully living in the heavenly kingdom where perfect justice reigns and serving Christ in this life may take the form of a doormat from time to time. In other words, persecute me for being a Christian, and I will let you with joy; persecute me for being a human being, and you will have a fight on your hands. . . and I'm a biter!

So, based on the above observations, was Harry correct in defending his family name with force? No. The image of God in neither Harry nor his mother was in danger of being threatened or destroyed. Harry merely wanted revenge. His anger was unrighteous. Instead of turning the other cheek, Harry submitted to his ungodly temper. If we are to be like Christ, we must ask ourselves if we desire revenge, or if we possess righteous anger. Suffering for Christ is a blessing, but suffering in an evil world is not a blessing, it's a curse. We must be willing to suffer for the name of Christ. However, we are also charged with the responsibility to defend and protect humanity because we carry the image of God.

---

[9] David VanDrunen, "Bearing Sword in the State, Turning Cheek in the Church: A Reformed Two-Kingdoms Interpretation of Matthew 5:38-42," *Themelios* 34, no. 3 (2009): 334.

4

HARRY POTTER AND THE HALF-BLOOD PRINCE

[After Watching *Harry Potter and the Half-Blood Prince*]

What Would You Do With Supernatural Power?

Throughout this movies series, Rowling presents various individuals who have supernatural abilities. Some use these abilities for good while others use them for evil. If you had such supernatural abilities, what would you do with them? For example, Dumbledore, who is arguably the most powerful wizard in the world, has virtually limitless power. If you possessed such power, what would you do with it? Would you use your powers for selfish reasons or for the purpose of loving God with all your heart, soul, and mind, and for loving your neighbor as yourself (Matt. 22:37-40)?

As we contemplate this question, do any sins come to mind? What would I do with the ability to teleport wherever I wanted? Would I think of using my gift to spread the love of God through Christ to the ends of the earth (Matt. 28:18-20), or would I use this gift to get in and out of bank vaults, in and out of locked stores, homes, etc.? If we would use such a gift for the purpose of fulfilling sinful desires, then we have not dealt with our wicked hearts. Our problem is not that we would teleport into bank vaults, if allowed, but that we *desire* to do so. Without the ability to teleport, we may be safe from the guilt of robbing banks; yet we are not safe from the guilt of selfishness and thievery.

Christians need to be more than just one opportunity away from sinful failure. It is for this reason that many men and, increasingly many women, are addicted to Internet pornography. Since fulfilling various sexual and emotional fantasies are merely one click away on the Internet, men and women suffer with this addiction. Years ago, these same men and women would never have gone to a store to buy pornography, but the anonymous nature of the Internet provides the *opportunity* to sin without the previous restrictions—fear of being caught, embarrassment, etc.—that hid the wicked hearts of these men and women. Upon further inspection of these men and women, the problem is the same: Christians must deal with their wicked hearts, or they are doomed for failure (Matt. 7:20-24).

If you and I are merely one opportunity from sinful failure, Satan, our flesh, or another sinner will probably provide that opportunity. Christianity, however, should run deeper than that; Christianity should run to our hearts. I once visited a man in prison who struggled with drug addiction. He had been clean from drugs for years prior to being in prison that time, but then he received a large sum of money which provided him an opportunity to buy any drug he wanted. He told me that when he got out of jail this time, he would have to be clean because he had no other choice. I told him that his trust in Christ should run deeper than "this is my only choice." I asked him what he would do if Satan handed him a million dollars. He lowered his head. That's what happens when you don't deal with your wicked heart. If Christ is not your treasure, then you have not dealt with your wicked heart.

The same can be said for the person who struggles with losing his temper. To tell if this person has dealt with his wicked heart concerning his anger, simply place him in a tense situation, and you will quickly see whether or not he has dealt with his wicked heart. Place this man in a traffic jam, in a room of screaming children, etc. You will quickly see the sad reality that the heart is deceitful above all things, and desperately sick, who can understand it (Jer. 17:9)? There are two possible answers for this man: he can try to avoid all tense situations and live as if the world is the problem, or he can deal with his wicked heart and glorify God while living in an evil world. In other words, he can either say, "*You* make me so mad," or, "*I'm* sorry for my unrighteous anger." Unfortunately, many men try to avoid all tense situations which enables them to falsely think they have dealt with their sin, but the Bible argues that sinners have a heart problem, not an external problem. So, what is the answer for those Christians who are one opportunity away from sinful failure?

The Answer for the wicked heart today is the same Answer since the Fall: Jesus Christ (John 14:6). When you contemplate evil in your mind, repent, get up, and savor God through Christ. Enjoy God through Christ, and seek to enjoy Him continually. Get out of the bed to enjoy Christ; go to work to enjoy Christ; go to school to enjoy Christ; go to the supermarket to enjoy Christ; go home to enjoy Christ; get married to enjoy Christ; have children to enjoy Christ, etc. It is impossible to enjoy God through pornography, drugs, materialism, idolatry, sexual immorality, lying, stealing, or any other sin our depraved minds can muster. We were created to enjoy God forever (Gen. 1-2), but since the Fall, we can only enjoy God fully through the death and resurrection of Jesus Christ. Are you enjoying God through Christ, or are you merely one opportunity away from sinful failure?

Must Christians Live Out Their Positions In Christ?

At around 00:29:30, Dumbledore explains that Lord Voldermort began as a student at Hogwarts named Tom Riddle. Dumbledore says,

> Today, of course, he's known all over the world by another name. Which is why as I stand looking out upon you all tonight, I'm reminded of a sobering fact: every day, every hour, this very minute perhaps, dark forces attempt to penetrate this castle's walls. In the end, their greatest weapon is you. Just something to think about.

Dumbledore is essentially saying, "Don't let the dark forces influence you!" Christians too must shout with Dumbledore to ourselves and other Christians as well, "Don't let the dark forces influence you!"

The Bible teaches there are two kingdoms: God's kingdom and the devil's kingdom (Gen. 3; especially Gen. 3:15). All humans belong to one or the other. Those who come to God through Christ are members of God's kingdom (John 14:6), while those who reject Christ are forever members of the devil's kingdom (Matt. 13:38-43; Eph. 2:1-7) and will burn eternally in hell as a result (Rev. 19:20, 20:10, 14, 15). God, however, has snatched Christians out of the devil's kingdom and placed us in His own. Therefore, we must live out our position in God's kingdom (Eph. 2:1-10). We must exercise the fruit of the

Spirit: love, joy, peace, patience, kindness, goodness, faithfulness, gentleness, and self-control (Gal. 5:22-23). To whose kingdom do you belong?

Is the Bible Inerrant?

At around 00:37:20, Dumbledore shows Harry a storage unit where memories of Tom Riddle are stored. Harry then views one of Tom's memories from "God's viewpoint," seeing the memory in real time as it took place many years before. Essentially, memories happening in real time are what Christians possess in the Scriptures:

> 2 Peter 1:21 – [21]For no prophecy was ever produced by the will of man, but men spoke from God as they were carried along by the Holy Spirit.
>
> 2 Timothy 3:16-17 – [16]All Scripture is breathed out by God and profitable for teaching, for reproof, for correction, and for training in righteousness, [17]that the man of God may be competent, equipped for every good work.

We witness the memories of various authors throughout history since these are written down for the church in both the Old and New Testaments. The difference is that the Scriptures possess accurate memories, uncorrupted by fallen humans, since they were carried along by God the Holy Spirit to write down the breathed out Word of God (2 Pet. 1:21; 2 Tim. 3:16-17). God used human authors, without negating their personalities, to write inerrant truth as they were inspired by God the Holy Spirit. Do you believe the Word of God based on its own statements about itself? If you do, then the Word of God should be more valuable to you than the opinions of men.

Should Christians Judge?

At around 00:20:30, Harry, Ron, and Hermione follow Malfoy to a secret meeting with Death Eaters. Harry, Ron, and Hermione then debate whether or not Draco Malfoy is now a Death Eater. Furthermore, at around 00:51:30, when discussing Katy being cursed, Harry says, "It was Malfoy." When asked for his evidence by Professor Snape, Harry says, "I just know." Is Harry's example accurate concerning how Christians should respond when making judgments about individuals? No.

First, Christ says, "Do not judge by appearances, but judge with right judgment" (John 7:24). In other words, do not judge based on appearance, but judge based on the Scriptures or truth. Specifically, Jesus was talking about the Pharisees being angry that He healed a man on the Sabbath (John 7:21-24). They were judging His act based on their own opinions of the truth, instead of based on the actual truth concerning the Sabbath, and Jesus's position as Lord of the Sabbath (Mark 2:28).

If Christians judge, we must judge based on truth. We must judge rightly, for if we judge wrongly, the measure we use will be measured to us (Matt. 7:1-2). Because we are sinners, we struggle with a great desire to see everyone's faults but our own (Matt. 7:1-5). We must look in the mirror before we judge others.

Should Christians Use Performance Enhancing Drugs as They Participate in Sports?

At around 00:58:30, Ron thinks he drinks a "good luck" potion before his Quidditch game. This potion, if real, would give Ron and his team an unfair advantage in the Quidditch game. Is it Biblically ethical to use performance enhancing substances to gain an advantage over your opponent in sports or other areas of life? No.

Throughout this Bible study, our basic moral guideline as Christians are the two greatest commandments: 1) Love the Lord your God with all your heart, soul, and mind; and 2) Love your neighbor as yourself (Matt. 22:37-40). When considering taking performance enhancing substances, we must do and think as a result of loving God and our neighbors. Thus, it is permissible to use a performance enhancing drug if the substance doesn't harm your body, and opponents can take the same substance as well. If your opponents do not have access, then consuming a substance provides an *unfair* advantage. There is no way we can love our neighbors, our opponents, as ourselves through cheating.

Furthermore, there's no way we can love God with all our hearts, souls, and minds by refusing to work hard (1 Tim. 5:18). The basic assumption of a man being worthy of his working wages is that he is paid in accordance with the amount and type of work he produces. If a man takes short cuts, cheats, lies, is lazy, etc., then his working wage is necessarily lower than another man who works as unto the Lord. Working hard with excellence glorifies God, but cheating and deceitfulness never glorify God. The desire to win above the desire to please God will send many to hell. There is only one name that echoes in eternity, "Jesus Christ," to the glory of God the Father (Phil. 2:9-11). Since the goal is to be with Him, let us play sports for the purpose of enjoying God through Jesus, instead of for the purpose of enjoying winning through sin.

Is Anything in Life Left up to "Chance?"

Again at around 01:18:20, Harry sees another memory dealing with Tom Riddle. This time, however, the memory is corrupted by Professor Slughorn. Dumbledore says, "This memory is everything. Without it, we are blind. Without it, we leave the fate of our world to chance. You have no choice. You must not fail." Is this ever true in real life? Is there anything left up to chance regardless what we do? No.

The Bible teaches God is in control of all things. Nothing is left up to "chance." All things, both good and evil, fit into God's sovereign plan from before time even existed:

> Deuteronomy 32:39 – ³⁹See now that I, even I, am he, and there is no god beside me; I kill and I make alive; I wound and I heal; and there is none that can deliver out of my hand.
>
> Isaiah 45:7 – ⁷I form light and create darkness, I make well-being and create calamity, I am the LORD, who does all these things.
>
> John 1:4-5 – ⁴In him was life, and the life was the light of men. ⁵The light shines in the darkness, and the darkness has not overcome it.
>
> Psalm 5:4 – ⁴For you are not a God who delights in wickedness; evil may not dwell with you.
>
> Acts 2:23 – ²³This Jesus, delivered up according to the definite plan and foreknowledge of God, you crucified and killed by the hands of lawless men.

The beginning and end of creation has been mapped out, and the choices both men and women make somehow fit into this map. God is one hundred percent sovereign and man is one hundred percent responsible (Acts 2:23; Matt. 18:7; Mark 14:21). These things are worked out in the mind of God, but, at the very least, we know "chance" doesn't exist. If you are a Christian, you should sleep well tonight knowing God is in control of all things. However, if you are not a Christian, you should never sleep again until you come to God through Christ. It is a fearful thing to fall into the hands of the living God (Heb. 10:31).

Is Telling Untruth Ever Permitted by God?

At around 01:24:25, Harry lies to Ron, telling him he will introduce him to Romilda Vane. He really intends to help Ron by taking him to Professor Slughorn to be cured from the deception of a love potion. Without Harry's lie, Ron would not be willing to receive help. Harry, for the sake of loving his neighbor, lies to Ron. What should Christians think about Harry's example?

I visit the nursing home often. Many elderly people suffer from brain degenerating diseases, such as Alzheimer's, Parkinson's, etc. Their families, nurses, doctors, and staff must continually tell these patients untruth for their own benefit. For the sake of loving their neighbors, these Christians must continually say untrue things. If you tell an Alzheimer's patient the truth, and he is mobile, down the hall he'll go, leaving the facility.

In other words, as we think through when it's permitted by God to tell someone something untrue as truth, we must allow the two greatest commandments to govern our decision: 1) Love the Lord your God with all your heart, soul, and mind; and 2) Love your neighbor as yourself (Matt. 22:37-40). Thus, Christians are free to present untrue things as truth, so long as they're loving their neighbors and God in doing so. [A more specific ethic for lying is covered in the Digging Deeper section of this chapter.]

Can Humans Have Their Best Lives Now?

At around 01:48:00, we see Professor Slughorn's true memory involving Tom Riddle. He reveals to Tom that it's possible to split one's soul apart from his body. The problem is that someone must be killed in order to do this. Murder, thus, breaks the soul apart. In an evil attempt to gain eternal life, Lord Voldermort was willing to murder seven people so his soul could be broken into seven pieces and placed in seven Horcruxes—magical objects that each would hold a piece of the soul. In other words, Lord Voldermort wanted eternal life in this world. Is living forever in a wicked world something that Christians should desire? No. Christians should desire to live apart from sin, not to live continually in a sinful world. Imagine living forever in an evil world. What a dreadful thought!

The sad reality is that this dreadful thought is the dream of billions. They literally love sin so much they're trading their souls to enjoy it (Mark 8:36). Even sadder is the further reality that sin is not satisfying them. They're exhausting one sin and running to another, all the while rejecting the only One who can give them who they desperately need: God. Having been created by God for the purpose of enjoying Him forever, humans have a God-shaped hole that can only be filled with their Creator.

Because of sin, humans try to fill this hole with things other than God, thus lacking the full enjoyment in God that Christ came to give (John 10:10).

Should Christians Be Afraid to Stand Against Evil?

Near the end of the movie, we see Harry's courage to face the evil that killed Dumbledore, the most powerful wizard on earth. What courage to stand against evil! Do you possess the same courage to stand against the evil one and his servants?

Harry had the assurance that he was the chosen one. Christians have the even greater assurance that if God is for them, who can be against them (Rom. 8:31-39)? We literally have nothing to fear since the fear of God is the beginning of wisdom (Prov. 9:10), and God is working all things out for our good, for those who love Him and are called according to His purpose (Rom. 8:28). Now, this truth doesn't mean that God is working things out for us necessarily the way we think He should, but that He knows what is good, and works according to His own will and plan. Thus, even when bad things happen in the Christian's life, however evil, sorrowful, heart-breaking they may be, these issues still fit into God's overarching plan to work all things out for our good. So, we should be unafraid to stand against evil.

Digging Deeper:
Should Christians Ever Be Dishonest?

At the beginning of the movie, Harry lies to the waitress about his identity. Their discussion becomes playful, but was Harry morally right to lie to this waitress? No. Lying is permitted by God whenever the lie affords an opportunity to protect the life of an individual. Remember that Jesus said the greatest commandment was for us to love the Lord our God with all our hearts, souls, and minds, and the second greatest commandment was to love our neighbors as ourselves (Matt. 22:37-39).

One Scriptural example of loving God and our neighbors above ourselves is found in Joshua 2 when Rahab the Prostitute lied in order to protect the spies of Israel:

> [1]And Joshua the son of Nun sent two men secretly from Shittim as spies, saying, "Go, view the land, especially Jericho." And they went and came into the house of a prostitute whose name was Rahab and lodged there. [2]And it was told to the king of Jericho, "Behold, men of Israel have come here tonight to search out the land." [3]Then the king of Jericho sent to Rahab, saying, "Bring out the men who have come to you, who entered your house, for they have come to search out all the land." [4]But the woman had taken the two men and hidden them. And she said, "True, the men came to me, but I did not know where they were from. [5]And when the gate was about to be closed at dark, the

men went out. I do not know where the men went. Pursue them quickly, for you will overtake them." ⁶But she had brought them up to the roof and hid them with the stalks of flax that she had laid in order on the roof. ⁷So the men pursued after them on the way to the Jordan as far as the fords. And the gate was shut as soon as the pursuers had gone out. ⁸Before the men lay down, she came up to them on the roof ⁹and said to the men, "I know that the LORD has given you the land, and that the fear of you has fallen upon us, and that all the inhabitants of the land melt away before you. ¹⁰For we have heard how the LORD dried up the water of the Red Sea before you when you came out of Egypt, and what you did to the two kings of the Amorites who were beyond the Jordan, to Sihon and Og, whom you devoted to destruction. ¹¹And as soon as we heard it, our hearts melted, and there was no spirit left in any man because of you, for the LORD your God, he is God in the heavens above and on the earth beneath. ¹²Now then, please swear to me by the LORD that, as I have dealt kindly with you, you also will deal kindly with my father's house, and give me a sure sign ¹³that you will save alive my father and mother, my brothers and sisters, and all who belong to them, and deliver our lives from death." ¹⁴And the men said to her, "Our life for yours even to death! If you do not tell this business of ours, then when the LORD gives us the land we will deal kindly and faithfully with you." ¹⁵Then she let them down by a rope through the window, for her house was built into the city wall, so that she lived in the wall. ¹⁶And she said to them, "Go into the hills, or the pursuers will encounter you, and hide there three days until the pursuers have returned. Then afterward you may go your way." ⁱ⁷The men said to her, "We will be guiltless with respect to this oath of yours that you have made us swear. ¹⁸Behold, when we come into the land, you shall tie this scarlet cord in the window through which you let us down, and you shall gather into your house your father and mother, your brothers, and all your father's household. ¹⁹Then if anyone goes out of the doors of your house into the street, his blood shall be on his own head, and we shall be guiltless. But if a hand is laid on anyone who is with you in the house, his blood shall be on our head. ²⁰But if you tell this business of ours, then we shall be guiltless with respect to your oath that you have made us swear." ²¹And she said, "According to your words, so be it." Then she sent them away, and they departed. And she tied the scarlet cord in the window. ²²They departed and went into the hills and remained there three days until the pursuers returned, and the pursuers searched all along the way and found nothing. ²³Then the two men returned. They came down from the hills and passed over and came to Joshua the son of Nun, and they told him all that had happened to them. ²⁴And they said to Joshua, "Truly the LORD has given all the land into our hands. And also, all the inhabitants of the land melt away because of us."

God had already promised Israel that the land of Canaan would be given to them. God's holiness was specifically associated with Israel at this time since Israel as a nation was His chosen people (Exod. 19:5-6). Rahab hid the Israelite spies because she had heard of God's miraculous provision for Israel and their dominance of other kingdoms (Josh. 2:10-12). Rahab possessed faith in Israel's God, saying, "...for the LORD your God, He is God in the heavens above and on the earth beneath" (Josh. 2:11). Since God's holiness was directly associated with Israel at this time, to protect Israel was to protect God's holiness. Thus, by telling untruth for the sake of God's people, Rahab revealed that she loved Israel's God with all her heart, soul, and mind (Matt. 22:39). Rahab is even included in the "Hall of Faith" found in Hebrews 11: "By faith Rahab the prostitute did not perish with those who were disobedient, because she had given a friendly welcome to the spies" (Heb. 11:31). She protected these men in obedience to God.

Although the situation is different for us today since no theocracies exist, the truth is that Scripture does allow for lies in very specific circumstances. In other words, the basic principle surrounding the two greatest commandments is that it is Biblically permissible to say something is not true even though it is true, if in doing so you reveal your love for God and your neighbor. Think about if you lived during WWII. Would you hide Jews from the Nazis? If you lived during the Britain and American slave trade, would you hide slaves from their abusive masters? What if you and your child were in your home and an intruder broke in, would you be justified to lie to the intruder about the location of your child? Absolutely!

The question then comes as to whether or not parents should try to protect their children from suffering for the name of Christ. I don't think there is a hard and fast rule, but I do think suffering for the sake of Christ is the decision of an individual, not a decision one person can make for someone else. In other words, if an intruder broke into my home hoping to hurt me because I am a Christian, then I would let him with joy. But if he asked where my family was, I would not tell him the truth. Now, each member of my family could come out and reveal himself or herself if he or she so chose, but it is not my decision to make for them.

5

HARRY POTTER AND THE DEATHLY HALLOWS - PART 1

[After Watching *Harry Potter and the Deathly Hallows - Part 1*]

How Should Christians Respond to Racism?

At the beginning of the movie, suspended upside down above the table at the meeting of the Dark Lord and his Death Eaters is Charity Burbage, a former teacher at Hogwarts. Her specialty was muggle studies: the study of those who don't possess magical ability and were not born into the magical world. She is tortured by Lord Voldermort because he hates muggles. If he had his way, the world would be only full of wizards and all muggles would be dead. He views the mixture of muggle and magical blood as an abomination. As a result of his hatred, he murders Ms.

Burbage in front of the other Death Eaters and feeds her to his snake. Draco Malfoy reacts in sorrow from witnessing this murder.

In response to this clear racism, Christians should make sure they do not possess even a hint of the extreme behavior and mentality exhibited by Lord Voldermort. The Bible does not diminish one race below another. All humans are fearfully and wonderfully made (Ps. 139:14), which does *not* mean *some* humans are more fearfully and more wonderfully made than others. Thus, the mixture of various human blood is not prohibited by God. In other words, God doesn't care if different races intermarry. However, He does care if Christians intermarry with non-Christians.

There are many Scriptures used by those against interracial marriage. The problem is almost all of these Scriptures come from the Old Testament as God commanded Israel to be a nation set apart from other nations. God was concerned about His people worshiping the gods of other nations, not about them marrying persons who were a different race than they were. Every nation or race God commanded the Israelites not to marry worshiped other gods. If God was speaking against interracial marriages, why did Moses marry an Ethiopian woman? His sister even spoke against him, and God smote her with leprosy (Num. 12:1-16).

It seems according to Scripture, God is more concerned with who we *don't* marry than who do we marry. In other words, we are free in Christ to marry any Christian person of the opposite sex we choose to covenant together with before God to determinately love until death do us part. We are not free to marry non-Christians. Thus, Christians shouldn't even date or court non-Christians:

> Deuteronomy 7:3-4 – ³You shall not intermarry with them, giving your daughters to their sons or taking their daughters for your sons, ⁴for they would turn away your sons from following me, to serve other gods. Then the anger of the LORD would be kindled against you, and he would destroy you quickly.
>
> 1 Corinthians 7:39 – ³⁹A wife is bound to her husband as long as he lives. But if her husband dies, she is free to be married to whom she wishes, only in the Lord.
>
> 2 Corinthians 6:14-16 – ¹⁴Do not be unequally yoked with unbelievers. For what partnership has righteousness with lawlessness? Or what fellowship has light with darkness? ¹⁵What accord has Christ with Belial? Or what portion does a believer share with an unbeliever? ¹⁶What agreement has the temple of God with idols? For we are the temple of the living God; as God said, "I will make my dwelling among them and walk among them, and I will be their God, and they shall be my people.

In the Old Testament, part of God's plan for Israel to remain faithful to Him when they entered the Promised Land was the requirement they only marry other worshipers of Yahweh (Deut. 7:3-4). We see similar commands in Scripture when Paul told widows they were free to marry whomever they wished, only in the Lord (1 Cor. 7:39). Paul, in 2 Corinthians, tells Christians they shouldn't be unequally yoked with unbelievers in anything (2 Cor. 6:14-16). The context is not necessarily speaking about marriage, but marriage would be included. If Christians aren't to join in business endeavors with unbelievers, surely we shouldn't marry unbelievers either. Paul's concern is with professed Christians leaving Christianity.

Furthermore, if you have married a non-Christian, you have still covenanted together with that person to determinately love him or her until death do you part. To those Christians who may be considering marrying a non-Christian, ask any Christian who has married a non-Christian, and you will hear how difficult it is to not share in your marriage relationship the reason why you live: your relationship with God. We date to enjoy God through Christ. We marry to enjoy God through Christ, but it is impossible to enjoy God through sin.

Should Christians Have Good Works?

At the beginning of the movie, the Order of the Phoenix hopes to protect Harry because he's the chosen one. They believe he's the one who was predetermined to defeat Lord Voldermort. Many friends step forward, risking their lives by transforming into the likeness of Harry for the purpose of saving him and for the sake of his eventual defeat of Lord Voldermort.

Just as Harry's friends backed up their beliefs with actions, Christians are expected to do the same. With contemporary Christianity today, there is a huge gap between what Christians say they believe and how they live. Unfortunately, what many Christians profess to believe affects how they live on a daily basis very little. What good are beliefs if there are no actions built on these beliefs? They are worthless.

James, the early church leader and half-brother of Jesus, wrote about this subject:

> [14]What good is it, my brothers, if someone says he has faith but does not have works? Can that faith save him? [15]If a brother or sister is poorly clothed and lacking in daily food, [16]and one of you says to them, "Go in peace, be warmed and filled," without giving them the things needed for the body, what good is that? [17]So also faith by itself, if it does not have works, is dead (James 2:14-17).

Faith without works is dead. This statement should startle and warn us. If we say we are Christians, we have come to God through Christ alone, repenting and believing (John 14:6), we affirm His death and resurrection (1 Cor. 15:1-4), we've been brought into right relationship with God through Jesus's finished work, we've received His Holy Spirit (Eph. 2:11-18), thus, admitting God Himself indwells us (Rom. 8:8-11), then we must live for Him, or we have a dead faith, a faith that isn't *saving* faith.

In other words, good works will not save you, but if you have been saved from God's wrath through faith in Jesus Christ, you will have good works (Rom. 7:4). Just like the man who gets hit by a car will never walk away the same as he was before, the sinner who has been born again by God the Father's work through Christ and the indwelling of God the Holy Spirit will never walk away the same either (Rom. 8:9). How can someone claim God indwells him or her and yet live like an unbeliever?

Should Christians Surround Themselves with Evil?

At around 01:16:00, Harry and Ron get into an argument due to the Horcrux around Ron's neck. Earlier we saw something similar happen with Harry due to the supernatural influence of the Horcrux. One must question if there are any parallels in the Christian's life today.

Scripture warns Christians about the influence of evil. Indeed, if a Christian voluntarily surrounds himself with evil, not for the purpose of exposing it, but for the purpose of enjoying it, he or she is doomed for failure eventually. Christians should *not* seek to enjoy evil. We must always be against evil as evidenced by our devotion to not tolerate sin, whether it be our own or someone else's.

The question of surrounding ourselves with evil provides us with the opportunity to examine whether or not we should have non-Christian friends, participate in non-Christian media (books, movies, music, TV, etc.), etc. First, Jesus was a friend of sinners (Luke 15:1-2). He was surrounded by sinful people at all times, including His disciples. Technically speaking, in an evil world, we cannot separate ourselves from sinful people, even if we only associate with Christians. It is for this reason the apostle Paul commands the Thessalonians not to despise prophecies (preaching), but to test everything, hold fast what is good, and abstain from every form of evil (1 Thess. 5:20-22). If preaching must never be despised, but always tested as we separate the good from the evil, then everything in the world must be tested with evil being hated and good being firmly grasped.

Second, just as Jesus was a friend of sinners, we too should be friends of sinners. Jesus wasn't influenced by these sinners but instead influenced many of them. At the very least, we should have non-Christian friends, but these non-Christian friends should not influence us. At the point they begin influencing us to be disobedient to God, we need to separate ourselves from them. Remember what Ron and Harry did when the Horcrux began influencing them? They took it off and moved it away from themselves, but, as mentioned earlier in this book, our outside influences are not the problem, the problem is our wicked hearts.

If non-Christian friends are influencing you, then you must deal with your wicked heart. You must question why you are valuing the opinions of your friends above being obedient to God. The answer is because you struggle with loving popularity, the opinions of men, etc. more than God. Jesus had non-Christian friends without being influenced by their disobedience. Jesus took every thought captive to obey His Father as He participated in an evil world (John 5:19).

Third, what about Christians participating in non-Christian media? Based on this book, I obviously believe Christians can participate in non-Christian media unto the glory of God. The reality is that we must dissect all we see and hear based on what the Scriptures say is true. As we participate in media we must reject some ideas, accept other ideas, and also connect half-truths to Scripture, adding truth where necessary to turn half-truths into whole truths. We cannot simply drink deeply of all forms of media as if God has not spoken the truth in His Word.

We must, instead, bring Scripture to bear on all media in which we participate, however, the moment this media begins influencing us, we need to stop participating in it until we have dealt with our wicked hearts. I don't know how many times I've seen professed Christians influenced by various forms of media because they started idolizing the media and its authors, instead of rightfully using media to enjoy God through Christ. The purpose of participating in anything in life, whether working, playing, eating, drinking, etc., is to enjoy God through Christ. Creation exists for the purpose of exalting its Creator (Ps. 19:1-6). To use creation for any other purpose than to enjoy God is idolatry. Media is no different as long as it contains some of God's fingerprints (proof of His image) and is not entirely evil. Therefore, in light of Christ, enjoy God through enjoying media.

How Should Christians Respond To Their Flesh and Satan?

There seems to be some jealousy from Ron toward the friendship of Harry and Hermione. Ron gets angry and leaves at one point, but returns at a later time and saves Harry from drowning. Ron then helps Harry destroy the Horcrux with the Sword of Gryffindor. Before he can deliver the deathblow, Voldemort's soul lies to Ron, showing him a hologram of Harry and Hermione kissing and telling Ron they were better without him. Ron responds exactly the way he should have responded: he overcomes his sin and the lies of the evil one, delivering a deadly blow to Voldemort's soul with the Sword of Gryffindor. This piece of Voldemort's soul dies instantly.

Christians can learn from Ron's example in light of their constant battle against sin and the evil one. The Bible indicates Christians are to treat their flesh and the evil one the same as Ron treated this Horcrux. We must put it to death! The apostle Paul communicated this reality in Romans 8:13: "For if you live according to the flesh you will die, but if by the Spirit you put to death the deeds of the body, you will live." Christians are involved in a holy war against both their flesh and the devil. We must rise up and fight!

First, how can we fight against Satan who is more powerful than we are? The answer is through submitting to God and resisting the devil (James 4:7). We cannot fight against the evil one on our own. We need God to bring the fight for us. This truth, however, does not eliminate our responsibility to put on the full armor of God.

In Ephesians 6:10-18 the apostle Paul spoke to the Christians in Ephesus concerning how to withstand Satan:

> [10]Finally, be strong in the Lord and in the strength of his might. [11]Put on the whole armor of God, that you may be able to stand against the schemes of the devil. [12]For we do not wrestle against flesh and blood, but against the rulers, against the authorities, against the cosmic powers over this present darkness, against the spiritual forces of evil in the heavenly places. [13]Therefore take up the whole armor of God, that you may be able to withstand in the evil day, and having done all, to stand firm.[14]Stand therefore, having fastened on the belt

of truth, and having put on the breastplate of righteousness, ⁱ⁵and, as shoes for your feet, having put on the readiness given by the gospel of peace. ¹⁶In all circumstances take up the shield of faith, with which you can extinguish all the flaming darts of the evil one; ¹⁷and take the helmet of salvation, and the sword of the Spirit, which is the word of God, ¹⁸praying at all times in the Spirit, with all prayer and supplication. To that end keep alert with all perseverance, making supplication for all the saints.

We must put on the whole armor of God. We are indeed in a battle against the evil one and all his armies. We must: 1) Know, believe, and hold fast to the truth because it holds all the armor together (v.14a). 2) Guard our feelings and emotions by putting on the righteousness of Christ (v.14b). 3) Firmly plant our feet with the gospel of peace, not slipping on false teaching (v.15). 4) Constantly have faith in Christ Jesus as He stands between us and Satan (v.16). 5) Keep the hope of our eternal salvation on our minds (v.17a). 6) Repel and attack Satan with the Sword of the Spirit, the Word of God (v.17b). 7) Always be dependent on God through prayer as we keep alert for the activity of the evil one (v.18). Are you willing to continually put on the whole armor of God so you may stand against the evil one (v.13)? Take the Sword of Gryffindor, I mean the Sword of the Spirit, and attack the evil one!

Second, if all Christians still live in sinful bodies after they're saved, then how can they live in holy obedience to the Lord? Christians must make war against their own flesh and its desires. The apostle Paul writes about this subject in Ephesians 4:17-24:

> [17]Now this I say and testify in the Lord, that you must no longer walk as the Gentiles do, in the futility of their minds. [18]They are darkened in their understanding, alienated from the life of God because of the ignorance that is in them, due to their hardness of heart. [19]They have become callous and have given themselves up to sensuality, greedy to practice every kind of impurity. [20]But that is not the way you learned Christ!—[21]assuming that you have heard about him and were taught in him, as the truth is in Jesus, [22]to put off your old self, which belongs to your former manner of life and is corrupt through deceitful desires, [23]and to be renewed in the spirit of your minds, [24]and to put on the new self, created after the likeness of God in true righteousness and holiness.

There is a real battle going on in every Christian's life between the flesh and the Spirit, and these two are opposed to each other (Gal. 5:16-17). Those who belong to Christ Jesus have crucified the flesh with its passions and desires (Gal. 5:24). If the Spirit has saved us, then God expects us to walk by the Spirit (Gal. 5:25). There were many evil things we did before we became Christians; but now we are commanded to put off these things and devote ourselves to full obedience since we have been changed by Christ (Col. 3:1-10). We are to work out our own salvation with fear and trembling, for it is the Lord who works in us to will and to work for His good pleasure (Phil. 2:12-13). Like disciplined athletes fighting for the prize, we must bring our flesh into submission so that when we share the good news of Jesus with others we do not discredit the gospel in their eyes (1 Cor. 9:24-27). We must declare war against the evil one and against our flesh; and we must intentionally fight every day!

Are Humans Valuable, Even in Death?

At around 02:11:30, Harry says he doesn't want to use magic to bury Dobby, but instead, wants to bury him "properly." Harry's desire for proper burial was a sign of respect for what Dobby did in giving his life for Harry and his friends. Harry also appears to love Dobby, to indeed possess a brotherly type love for him. Throughout the movie, human life is given a high value. Although Dobby is an elf, in Biblical terms, he still possesses the various elements that make up the image of God in humanity. He is obviously creative, emotional, moral, rational, relational, etc. Dobby, too, lives in our God's world and exhibits innate, human desires throughout his various appearances in the *Harry Potter* series. This provides us with an opportunity to think through the value of human bodies after death.

Have you ever been to a funeral? If so, were you amazed at the care given to a human body that no longer possessed any form of life? You probably weren't amazed because you have a great desire to value deceased humans as well. The reason why we believe humans are valuable in death is because all humans are created in God's image (Gen. 1:26). Even though our loved ones have left their bodies and this world, we still care very much for them as proven through how we treat them in burial. One must ask why we take such care of the dead. The answer is simply that all humans inherently believe humans are more valuable than animals. Often, regardless of religious persuasion, because humans value other humans more than animals, the deceased are given great care in their burial. In other words, all humans live in our God's world, and thus, desire to live out the reality that humans are valuable (created in God's image) even in death.

Digging Deeper:
Are Humans Valuable, Even In Times of War?

When Harry, Hermione, and Ron are attacked by two Death Eaters in the diner, Ron questions whether or not to kill them. They decide to merely erase their memories. Should Ron have desired to kill these Death Eaters?

The correct answer is not an easy one. Remember, as we discussed earlier, a basic Christian ethic to live by are the two greatest commandments: 1) Love the Lord your God with all your heart, soul, and mind; and 2) Love your neighbor as yourself. Therefore, based on Ron's desire to kill these two Death Eaters, was he being obedient to the above two commandments? No.

Ron wanted revenge, not justice. Harry answered correctly when he suggested to merely erase the Death Eaters' memories instead of killing them (even though his motive is difficult to know). Here are some questions to ask in order to apply the two greatest commandments to the above scenario: 1) Was the image of God in danger of being murdered in any individual when Ron asked about killing the Death Eaters? 2) Does Ron know the future concerning these Death Eaters? 3) Are prisoners of war, which are essentially what these two Death Eaters were at this moment since they were rendered helpless, less than human? The answer to all of these questions is "No."

Ron, Hermione, and Harry made the right decision in erasing the memories of the Death Eaters since they possibly protected each other's lives by loving their neighbors as themselves, while also protecting the image of God in these Death Eaters, allowing them to live without hurting other people. If the war between Lord Voldermort and the Order of the Phoenix ended within a few hours after Ron, Hermione, and Harry killed these Death Eaters, then they wouldn't have saved any lives through this execution. In other words, they didn't know the future, and they're not the judge and jury either. These men, no doubt, committed war crimes, but war crimes often depend on who wins the war, unless an enemy is killed without sufficient cause which is murder.

Also, please note this issue is not cut and dry. It is possible with such supernatural powers, these Death Eaters would need to be executed on site for the sake of justice and the protection of potential victims, especially muggles. Furthermore, it is also possible Harry's status as the chosen one, or as the leader of Dumbledore's Army, gave him the right to weigh and execute judgment upon the enemy on the battlefield even if he or others weren't in imminent danger.

Digging Deeper:
How Should Christians Respond to Sexuality In Media?

In the scene around 01:40:00 Lord Voldermort lies to Ron, showing him an image of Harry and Hermione kissing. It appears the two are nude. This unnecessary graphic scene gives us an opportunity to examine how Christians should respond to the inclusion of sexuality in media.

The Bible is clear: Christians are supposed to view only their spouses in a sexual way. When a nude scene or insinuated scene comes on the screen, or a man or woman on a commercial wears something that encourages lust, simply look away and treasure the truth of God hidden in your heart (Ps. 119:11). The body is not meant for sexual immorality, but for the Lord (1 Cor. 6:13).

Moreover, viewing a sex scene is wicked! It is the only act we are Biblically unable to look upon; to see someone other than our spouses in a sexual situation is evil. We are only supposed to see one man or one woman in a sexual situation our entire lives (Gen. 2:24; Matt. 5:27-28).

Also, it must be noted here if you don't deal with your wicked heart concerning this issue, you will *not* look away when a man or woman is scantily clad at work, the beach, swimming pool, school, supermarket, etc. Deal with your wicked heart by praying, running to the cross continually, memorizing Scripture, exercising self-control, because a woman or man dressed for the purpose of encouraging lust is in your near future, since you live in a wicked world. Satan, as well, will tempt you to seek marital intimacy, even if it's non-sexual, outside of your marriage, which is a form of adultery as well. Second only to our relationship with God, our marriage relationship is the most important relationship on earth.

Additionally, the reason why I emphasized humans only seeing one person in a "sexual situation" their entire lives, instead of arguing humans can only see one person nude their entire lives, is because of the reality that nudity is unavoidable if you're a parent or you're involved in certain professions. I see nude humans, other than my wife, on a daily basis because I change the diapers of my children. Furthermore, I have two sisters who are nurses, and they must see nude people constantly in their profession. Once again though, my sisters and I only see our own spouses in a sexual situation. How do we determine when it is Biblically permitted to uncover the nudity of another human being?

Remember our test for basic Christian ethics: 1) Am I loving the Lord my God with all my heart, soul, and mind? 2) Am I loving my neighbor as myself? With these two realities in mind, I must uncover the nakedness of my children for they are my neighbors, so they don't get diaper rashes, diseases, etc. My sisters must uncover the nakedness of various patients for the sake of their health. So, as a test case, what if you were the first person on the scene of a major car wreck where clothes were torn and an individual's nakedness was exposed? According to Scripture, how should you respond? The Biblical answer is you'd better love God and your neighbor through Christ by helping this person!

6

HARRY POTTER AND THE DEATHLY HALLOWS - PART 2

[After Watching *Harry Potter and the Deathly Hallows - Part 2*]

What is the Definition of Lying?

Griphook, the goblin, leaves Harry, Ron, and Hermione in the cave of Gringotts Wizarding Bank saying, "I told you I would get you in, but I didn't say I would help you out." He then leaves them to be captured or to die. Griphook acted like he did not deceive these three, but is he correct? No.

Concerning honesty, we must ask if allowing someone to wrongly assume something is true when it is not, is a lie. The simple answer is "yes." Of course, Harry, Ron, and Hermione assumed Griphook would help them get in *and out* of the bank vault. Any form of deception, regardless of how hidden, legal, less untruthful, etc. it may be, is still considered lying. God does not deceive in any form or fashion, and we are commanded to be holy for He is holy (1 Pet. 1:13-16). The definition of lying does not come from a goblin in *Harry Potter*, but from the Bible.

In Acts 5, we find the story of Ananias and Sapphira. At this time in the early church, the twelve apostles carried authority directly from Christ as the foundation layers of the church with Christ as the chief cornerstone (Eph. 2:20). Thus, to deceive them was to deceive God.

There were some Christians at this time who were selling various possessions in order to provide for the ministry of the church. One Christian named Ananias, with the knowledge of his wife, sold a piece of property and kept some of the money for himself, only giving a portion to the apostles. Ananias allowed everyone to think he was giving *all* the money he received from the sale to the church. Peter, however, viewed Ananias's intentional withholding of some truth and his intentional allowance of others to believe untruth, as *intentional* lying. Since the apostles had authority from Christ on earth, Ananias had not merely lied to men, but to God (Acts 5:3-4). Therefore, Ananias immediately died (Acts 5:5).

About three hours later, his wife came, and Peter asked her if she had sold the land for the amount her husband said, and she replied "Yes" (Acts 5:7-8). Peter questioned her lying and then told her those who buried her husband would also carry her out, and she died (Acts 5:9-10). What is the moral of this historical event? Deception is lying, regardless of what form it is presented in, whether we allow false assumptions, exaggerate, don't do what we said we would, etc. We must make sure whoever we're communicating with understands the whole truth we're communicating. Christians must be intentional to always tell the truth without any hint of deception, for even a little deception breaks God's command for Christians not to lie.

Should Christians Fear God More Than Satan?

Lord Voldermort speaks to all the students at around 00:37:00, telling them to give up Harry Potter to save their own lives. What would you have done? Would you have been selfish, or would you have loved your neighbor as yourself?

In similar manner, we must wonder if Satan tempted the other apostles to betray Christ like he did Judas. We can speculate continually, but at the very least, we must say Satan was at work throughout the lives of these individuals. Jesus told Peter Satan desired to sift him like wheat (Luke 22:31). Satan is at work in the lives of Christians today, as well, like a lion seeking people to devour (1 Pet. 5:8).

The sad reality is we are all like Judas or like the other apostles. We are either followers of Christ or betrayers of Christ. Our lives reveal the truth. Do you belong to God through Christ, and thus, you're fighting constantly against the evil one, or are you a member of Satan's kingdom?

In the book of Job, we find Satan interacting with God. God asks Satan, "Have you considered my servant, Job, that there is none like him on the earth, a blameless and upright man, who fears God and turns away from evil?" (Job 1:8). Satan replies,

> [9]Does Job fear God for no reason? [10]Have you not put a hedge around him and his house and all that he has, on every side? You have blessed the work of his hands, and his possessions have increased in the land. [11]But stretch out your hand and touch all that he has, and he will curse you to your face (Job 1:9-11).

Here Satan argues two things: 1) Job is not really righteous. 2) God is not worth worshiping apart from His blessings. But we know God is valuable enough in and of Himself to be worshiped. He is worthy of worship whether or not He has blessed anyone.

So, Satan is making negative statements about both Job and God. God responds, "Behold, all that he has is in your hand. Only against him do not stretch out your hand"

(Job 1:12). Satan is permitted by God to take everything Job loves on earth except Job himself.

Satan leaves the presence of God and attacks Job's children, possessions, and servants. He destroys almost all of them (Job 1:13-19). Job responds correctly, however, saying, "Naked I came from my mother's womb, and naked shall I return. The LORD gave, and the LORD has taken away; blessed be the name of the LORD" (Job 1:21). What we must recognize is even though Satan was permitted by God to take everything Job had except Job himself, he freely chose to spare the life of Job's wife. Why would Satan, a murderer and a liar (John 8:44), choose to spare the life of a human being he hates?

Satan evidently believed Job's wife was more valuable to him alive than dead. Based on what the Scriptures say, Satan seemed to be correct. After Job praised the Lord for giving and taking away, Satan requested to do more harm to Job, which the Lord allowed except Satan couldn't take Job's life (Job 2:6). After Job was afflicted by Satan with a disease (Job 2:1-8), Job's wife said to him, "Do you still hold fast your integrity? Curse God and die" (Job 2:9). Satan has no reason to kill those who belong to him. If Satan was permitted by God today to take any of us out of this world, would he consider us to be more valuable to him dead than alive? In other words, do we belong to Satan's kingdom or God's kingdom, or maybe, do we live as if we belong to Satan's kingdom even though we profess to belong to God's kingdom through Christ? If Satan was permitted by God today to take our lives, we should long to be more valuable to the evil one dead than alive, because we are actively fighting against his kingdom. Does Satan consider you an ally or an enemy?

Does the Majority Determine What is True?

At around 00:48:00, Professor Lupin says, "It is the quality of one's convictions that determines success, not the number of followers." Is this a true statement? If we think deeply about how many followers Christ truly had, based on sheer numbers, He would be labeled a failure if the above statement isn't true. However, if the quality of one's convictions determines success, or in other words "the truthfulness of one's convictions determines success," then Christ was indeed successful.

Moreover, all people who share truth and stand for truth are successful regardless of how many people stand with them. In today's society, if you follow the opinions of the majority, simply because they're the majority, then you are deceived. The opinions of the majority today change at the speed of the Internet and social media: Facebook, Twitter, Google+, etc. Christians, however, should not be tossed to and fro by the waves and carried about by every wind of doctrine (Eph. 4:14).

Do Sinners Deserve to be Saved from Their Sins?

At around 01:00:00, Harry and Ron go back for Draco Malfoy and save him from the fire that would have definitely killed him, even though he obviously didn't deserve to be saved based on his actions. Malfoy was part of Lord Voldermort's army, and he had just tried to kill Harry and Ron. Harry shows grace toward Malfoy. Does their merciful act remind you of anything?

Jesus indeed saved undeserving sinners through His death and resurrection. Even though we were guilty and deserved to eternally experience God's wrath in hell, Christ showed us mercy by taking our hell on the cross. On that cross, God withdrew His mercy from Jesus, pouring out His wrath on Him instead, causing Christ to cry out, "My God, my God, Why have you forsaken Me?" (Mark 15:34). Jesus was forsaken so all those who come to God through Him would be forgiven (Eph. 2:8-9), and God sent Jesus for this purpose. Have you experienced the *amazing* grace of God through Christ?

Does Satan Love Any Human?

At around 1:07:00, Lord Voldermort kills Professor Snape because he thought he couldn't truly possess the power of the Elder Wand as long as Professor Snape was alive. Lord Voldermort was completely selfish. He didn't care about anyone but himself and his own agenda. Satan is the same way.

In today's world, it's amazing how many people are willing to follow Satan instead of God. Satan does not care about his followers in the least. God even told Satan following his deception of Eve, "I will put enmity between you and the woman" (Gen. 3:15a). Satan is entirely selfish, and he hates all humanity.

Jesus argued that those who hate Him, hate His Father also (John 15:23). John the apostle also argued "²³No one who denies the Son has the Father. Whoever confesses the Son has the Father also" (1 John 2:23). Therefore, those who refuse to serve God through Christ automatically serve the evil one, even though he hates them (John 8:44). The only Way to have a relationship with God the Father is through God the Son. So, all those who reject Jesus automatically embrace Satan. Why are people choosing to serve Satan, who hates them, instead of serving God, who showed His love to them by crucifying His only Son (Acts 2:23)? It sounds ridiculous and crazy, yet billions choose the devil's kingdom over God's kingdom.

Is There Life Beyond this World?

At around 01:30:00, after Voldermort kills Harry, he goes to a place beyond this world. He sees a piece of Voldermort's soul there and Professor Dumbledore tells Harry he cannot help the soul for it was sent there to die. Rowling is correct in emphasizing the reality that there is a world beyond this world where humans are held accountable for how they lived on earth. As a result of our lives on earth, we will spend eternity in one of two places: heaven or hell.

The problem with humanity is since we are all sinners, our works can only earn us physical death, spiritual death, and eternal death (Rom. 3:23, 6:23). Thus, since we're judged based on our works, the whole human race is doomed to burn in hell forevermore… but God shows His love for us in that while we were yet sinners, Christ died for us (Rom. 5:8). In other words, sinners do not have to face God's wrath in hell since Jesus died to reconcile them to His Father (Col. 1:21-23). Jesus satisfied His Father's wrath toward sinners so those who come to God through Him will not experience any of God's wrath toward sin and sinners (1 John 4:10).

It is interesting that in this place where Harry and Dumbledore converse, Harry doesn't need glasses and isn't in pain due to Voldermort's deathblow. He doesn't appear to suffer any pains or shortcomings from his earthly experience. Even Dumbledore isn't in pain due to Professor Snape's deathblow. The piece of Lord Voldermort's soul, however, *is in pain*. There is indeed a world apart from this world where the wicked will be punished eternally and the righteous will be with God forever through Christ. Do you know where you're going when you leave this world?

What is the Purpose of Life?

At around 01:33:30, Dumbledore says, "Do not pity the dead Harry, pity the living, and above all, all those who live without love." In a Christian context, what a true statement! The Bible says God is love (1 John 4:8, 16). Thus, to know God is to know love. However, the only way to know God's love as a son or daughter is through His Son Jesus Christ (Luke 20:34-38; John 12:36). Those who do not know Jesus Christ do not know God beyond a general knowledge of Him—creation, conscience, etc.—which all humans possess (Rom. 1). Christians, however, experience God's *intimate* love through Christ (John 14:21, 23).

Furthermore, we must long for everyone to experience God's intimate love as well (Matt. 28:18-20). The main theme of *Harry Potter* is true, "Love conquers all." However, as revealed in Scripture, the love which conquers all is not mere human love, but is the love of God! This love is primarily revealed through God giving His Son to reconcile sinners to Himself (John 3:16; Rom. 5:8).

Returning to Dumbledore's quote above, he did not speak about God's love, but about love in general between friends and family. The love of family and friends is important, but experiencing their love is not the ultimate goal of love. Humans were created to enjoy God, and all creation exists for the purpose of humanity enjoying God (Gen. 1-2). Therefore, we experience the love of friends and family *so* we can enjoy God through the love of friends and family. Having created all things for His own glory, God is the source of all love (Gen. 1). So, let us enjoy God through Christ as we enjoy the love of friends and family!

Does Every Human Have Faith?

At around 01:38:00, Lord Voldermort says, "Harry Potter...is dead!" Ginny yells, "No!" Lord Voldermort exclaims, "Silence!" and then replies, "Stupid girl. Harry Potter is dead. From this day forth you put your faith in me." Does this sound familiar? I'm curious if Satan was thinking the same thing when Jesus died on the cross.

After Jesus began His earthly ministry, he chose twelve disciples. One of these men was named Judas Iscariot. He is one of the most famous disciples today because he betrayed Jesus Christ into the hands of the Roman soldiers. Right before Judas betrayed Jesus, Satan entered him so he could "bruise Jesus's heel" (Gen. 3:15; John 13:27). From the beginning in the Garden, and even in the temptation of Christ, Satan encouraged humans to put their faith in him instead of in God. Satan succeeded with Adam and Eve (Gen. 3:1-6), but Jesus the Last Adam (Rom. 5:12-21) never wavered (Matt. 4:1-11):

> Genesis 3:1-6 – [1]Now the serpent was more crafty than any other beast of the field that the LORD God had made. He said to the woman, "Did God actually say, 'You shall not eat of any tree in the garden'?" [2]And the woman said to the serpent, "We

may eat of the fruit of the trees in the garden, ³but God said, 'You shall not eat of the fruit of the tree that is in the midst of the garden, neither shall you touch it, lest you die.'" ⁴But the serpent said to the woman, "You will not surely die. ⁵For God knows that when you eat of it your eyes will be opened, and you will be like God, knowing good and evil." ⁶So when the woman saw that the tree was good for food, and that it was a delight to the eyes, and that the tree was to be desired to make one wise, she took of its fruit and ate, and she also gave some to her husband who was with her, and he ate.

Matthew 4:1-11 – ¹Then Jesus was led up by the Spirit into the wilderness to be tempted by the devil. ²And after fasting forty days and forty nights, he was hungry. ³And the tempter came and said to him, "If you are the Son of God, command these stones to become loaves of bread." ⁴But he answered, "It is written, "'Man shall not live by bread alone, but by every word that comes from the mouth of God.'" ⁵Then the devil took him to the holy city and set him on the pinnacle of the temple ⁶and said to him, "If you are the Son of God, throw yourself down, for it is written, "'He will command his angels concerning you,' and "'On their hands they will bear you up, lest you strike your foot against a stone.'" ⁷Jesus said to him, "Again it is written, 'You shall not put the Lord your God to the test.'" ⁸Again, the devil took him to a very high mountain and showed him all the kingdoms of the world and their glory. ⁹And he said to him, "All these I will give you, if you will fall

> down and worship me." ¹⁰Then Jesus said to him, "Be gone, Satan! For it is written,"' You shall worship the Lord your God and him only shall you serve.'" ¹¹Then the devil left him, and behold, angels came and were ministering to him.

Like Lord Voldermort, Satan selfishly wants to reign supreme over all humanity. He desires the faith of all, so long as they don't put their faith in the Triune God. He wants our allegiance, and we must realize if our allegiance is not to God through Jesus Christ, then we are putting our faith in the evil one. We are either sons and daughters of God through Christ, or we're sons and daughters of the evil one (Matt. 13:38-39).

Was Jesus Treated Like a Sinner?

Harry had to die because a piece of Voldermort, a piece of evil, was part of him. Jesus Christ, in similar manner, had to die because sin was placed on him. Paul, in 2 Corinthians 5:21 communicates this reality: "²¹For our sake he made him to be sin who knew no sin, so that in him we might become the righteousness of God." In order to conquer sin, its results, and the evil one, Jesus had to die. He yielded His life to the curse for three days, then rose from the dead, conquering the evil one, and all the results of sin (John 12:31-32; Heb. 2:14). It is for this reason Jesus is the only Way to overcome the results of the Fall. We must come to God through Him.

The results of the Fall plague humanity. Hunger, disease, storms, etc. exist because we're no longer in the Garden of Eden anymore because of sin and sinners. Through Jesus's virgin birth, He was revealed as God the Son incarnate (Matt. 1:23; John 1:1). By His perfect life, He was revealed as greater than Adam (Rom. 5). Through His miracles He was revealed as the Overcomer of the Fall, the Answer for the sin problem. As a result of Him casting out demons, He was revealed as the Crusher of the serpent's head (Gen. 3:15; Matt. 8:28-34). Through His resurrection, He was revealed as the ultimate Prophet, Priest, and King (Acts 3:22-23; Eph. 5:2; Heb. 6:20; Matt. 27:11; Mark 1:14-15). Jesus was treated like a sinner, so that all believers would be treated like sons and daughters. He is the only Answer for the sin problem, for "there is no other name under heaven given among men by which we must be saved" (Acts 4:12).

Did Jesus Defeat Death?

Near the end of the movie, Harry rose from the dead. He then defeated Lord Voldermort with the help of his friends. Jesus too rose from the dead, but He didn't have any "help" from His friends in defeating the evil one. Jesus, however, was not alone in His resurrection:

> Hebrews 13:20a – [20]Now may the God of peace who brought again from the dead our Lord Jesus.

> John 10:18 – ¹⁸No one takes it from me, but I lay it down of my own accord. I have authority to lay it down, and I have authority to take it up again. This charge I have received from my Father.

> 1 Peter 3:18 – ¹⁸For Christ also suffered once for sins, the righteous for the unrighteous, that he might bring us to God, being put to death in the flesh but made alive in the spirit.

The Trinity raised Jesus from the dead. Notice God the Father is said to have raised Jesus in Hebrews 13:20; God the Son is said to have raised Himself in John 10:18; and God the Holy Spirit is said to have made Christ alive after death in 1 Peter 3:18.

Moreover, Jesus conquered the wages of sin—death (Rom. 6:23). His actual resurrection defeated death, Satan, the curse, etc. Furthermore, this finished work of Christ prepared the way for others to be with Him forever in heaven (John 14:2-6). If you come to God through Christ you too will defeat death through Him. The apostle Paul speaks of this wonderful reality in 1 Corinthians 15:55-57:

> ⁵⁵'O death, where is your victory? O death, where is your sting?' ⁵⁶The sting of death is sin, and the power of sin is the law. ⁵⁷But thanks be to God, who gives us the victory through our Lord Jesus Christ.

If you are in Christ, physical death on this earth is a stingless process. We merely take our last breath here and our next breath in glory!

Is Jesus Different from Other "Sons of God" in the Bible?

Finally, instead of keeping the Elder Wand and guaranteeing his reign as the world's most powerful magician, Harry breaks the wand and throws it away. The main point we should gather from this act is Harry Potter is *not* Lord Voldermort. In similar manner, Jesus Christ is *not* like Satan or sinful humanity. Jesus Christ transcends or is "other" than us in holiness and love.

To summarize, when compared to various sons of God in Scripture, Jesus is the true Adam, coming to restore what Adam destroyed (Rom. 5:12-21). He is the true Israel, facing temptation in the wilderness, but continuing in perfect obedience to His Father (Matt. 4:1-11). He is the true David, reigning on his throne eternally (Matt. 22:41-46). He is the *true* Son of God as compared to all the sons of God throughout Biblical history who sinned: Adam, Noah, Abraham, Moses, Israel, David, Solomon, etc. All the evil, disease, pain, suffering, and death that surrounds us causes all humans to cry out for a Savior. God has heard and answered our cry through giving His only Son (John 3:16). Will you enjoy God through Jesus Christ, THE Son of God?

Digging Deeper:
Are our Deceased Loved Ones Still With Us?

At around 01:26:00, we see those who have died for Harry throughout his adventure. Voldermort won't be able to see them as Harry does, since these people are still with Harry in his heart. Is this true?

We need to be careful here as we examine where our loved ones go once they leave this world. The Bible argues as soon as we die we either go to heaven or hell (Luke 23:43; Luke 16:22-23; 2 Cor. 5:8-10). Thus, regardless of how much it may comfort us, we should be able to enjoy the wonderful fact our deceased loved ones are no longer with us in this evil world, but are with Christ in Paradise (if they were believers). We do also have the assurance that one day we will enjoy God through Christ forevermore with our deceased loved ones who died in Christ:

> Luke 23:43 – [43]And he said to him, "Truly, I say to you, today you will be with me in Paradise."

> Luke 16:22-23 – [22]The poor man died and was carried by the angels to Abraham's side. The rich man also died and was buried, [23]and in Hades, being in torment, he lifted up his eyes and saw Abraham far off and Lazarus at his side.

> 2 Corinthians 5:8-10 – [8]Yes, we are of good courage, and we would rather be away from the body and at home with the Lord. [9]So whether we are at home or away, we make it our aim to please

him. ¹⁰For we must all appear before the judgment seat of Christ, so that each one may receive what is due for what he has done in the body, whether good or evil.

In each of these Scripture references, there seems to be immediate judgment once humans die. We either go to a place of comfort or a place of torment.

Moreover, it must be mentioned here we often do not know who truly trusts in Christ and who does not. So, don't speculate concerning the location of your deceased loved ones. If they were not believers near death that you knew of, they may have trusted in Christ before death without your knowledge.

According to Scripture, there were two thieves crucified next to Jesus. At one point, *both* of these thieves mocked Jesus (Matt. 27:44). Only a few hours later, one of the thieves placed his faith and trust in Jesus Christ as God the Son (Luke 23:39-43). Jesus told this man "today, you will be with me in Paradise" (Luke 23:43). This man had a deathbed confession, and yet he's in heaven with Christ today. The same may be said for some of our loved ones who knew the gospel and possibly trusted in Christ at the last moment.

APPENDIX 1: IN FAVOR OF CHRISTIANS WATCHING SCARY MOVIES

I know many women, and I assume many men, struggle with watching scary movies or TV shows. When they watch something scary, they *allow* it to scare them to the point they doubt God's sovereignty as a "result." They, thus, limit their Christian freedom by refusing to participate in scary media. I do *not* think such people should violate their consciences, but I *do* think they should *better* inform their consciences.

First, if you doubt God, scary movies are *not* the reason; rather, scary movies merely bring to the surface the doubt that is *already* there in your heart. If you cannot watch scary movies *without* doubting that God is in control of all things, what will you do when scary situations come to your doorstep, unannounced and uninvited? The answer is you *will* doubt God yet again because you have foolishly thought the problem was *outside* of you. Your heart (will, mind, thoughts, virtually everything about you) is the problem, *not* scary movies (Jer. 17:9; Mark 7:17-23; Rom. 3:23).

In limiting your Christian freedom by refusing to watch scary movies, you assume the problem is *external*, when in reality, the problem is *internal*. Until you deal with your doubting heart—your fear of man, demons, or the unknown *above* the fear of God—you will *not* be filled with the Spirit in this area of your life. When you face scary situations, such as disease, illness, broken bones, surgery, physical harm, mental harm, etc., you *will* doubt the Lord all over again because you have *not* dealt with the problem: your heart.

The answer to your sin problem is not attempting to minimize your outside influences. You *should* be able to face scary situations, whether voluntary or involuntary, *without* doubting God. Rather, your answer should be to pray, memorize Scripture, and face voluntary fears while *believing* what God has said in His perfect Word. Like David, we must treasure the Word of God in our hearts so we might not sin against God (Ps. 119:11).

Finally, for those reading these words who are clinically depressed, I want you to know a doubting heart is *not* a disease, but is rather a sinful *choice*. Although there will be elements of your depression that *are* out of your control (still hotly debated today in Christian and secular counseling), you must make sure you *are* controlling what you are *able* to control. Remind yourself of the truth found in God's Word: "The fear of the Lord is the beginning of wisdom" (Prov. 9:10), "do not be anxious about anything, but in everything by prayer and supplication with thanksgiving let your requests be made known to God" (Phil. 4:6). I've known godly Christians who were clinically depressed to the point of continual physical pain. There are many elements of their depression they *cannot* control, but some elements they can. Don't give up. Work on what you are able to control.

Finally, we must make sure we deal with our wicked hearts. Concerning humanity's heart problem, David Powlison writes, "The core insanity of the human heart is that we violate the first great commandment. We will love anything, except God, unless our madness is checked by grace."[10] This includes loving the appearance of safety more than God and trusting our own ability to avoid scary things than the actual gospel itself which saves us from this scary world. A Christian who refuses to participate in media may be doing nothing righteous for himself *if* he does not deal with his wicked heart. The answer to our doubting hearts is *not* to limit our Christian freedom, but rather to 1) run to Christ, 2) trust in His finished work alone for our salvation and sanctification, 3) treasure His inerrant Word, 4) believe it beyond our outside and inside influences, and 5) trust Him to rule our hearts for all eternity.

How will you respond?

[10] David Powlison, "What is Sin?" *The Journal of Biblical Counseling* 25, no. 2 (Spring 2007): 25-26.

BIBLIOGRAPHY

Bauckham, Richard. *Jesus and the God of Israel: God Crucified and Other Studies on the New Testament's Christology of Divine Identity*. Grand Rapids: Eerdmans, 2008.

Dods, Marcus, ed. *The Works of Aurelius Augustine, Bishop of Hippo: A New Translation, Vol. IX – On Christian Doctrine; The Enchiridion; On Catechising; and On Faith and the Creed*. Edinburgh: T. & T. Clark, 1892.

Frame, John. "Presuppositional Apologetics." In *Five Views on Apologetics*, edited by Stanley N. Gundry and Steven B. Cowan, 207-231. Grand Rapids: Zondervan, 2000.

González, Justo L. *The Story of Christianity: The Early Church to the Dawn of the Reformation*. San Francisco: Harper & Row, 1984.

Pearcey, Nancy. *Total Truth: Liberating Christianity from Its Cultural Captivity*. Wheaton, Ill: Crossway Books, 2004.

Powlison, David. "What is Sin?" *The Journal of Biblical Counseling* 25, no. 2 (Spring 2007): 25-26.

Rowling, J.K., Michael Goldenberg, Daniel Radcliffe, Emma Watson, and Rupert Grint. *Harry Potter and the Order of the Phoenix*. DVD. Directed by David Yates. Burbank, CA: Warner Bros. Pictures, 2007.

Rowling, J.K., Steve Kloves, Daniel Radcliffe, Emma Watson, and Rupert Grint. *Harry Potter and the Half-Blood Prince*. DVD. Directed by David Yates. Burbank, CA: Warner Bros. Pictures, 2009.

Rowling, J.K., Steve Kloves, Daniel Radcliffe, Emma Watson, and Rupert Grint. *Harry Potter and the Deathly Hallows - Part 1*. DVD. Directed by David Yates. Burbank, CA: Warner Bros. Pictures, 2010.

Rowling, J.K., Steve Kloves, Daniel Radcliffe, Emma Watson, and Rupert Grint. *Harry Potter and the Deathly Hallows - Part 2*. Film. Directed by David Yates. Burbank, CA: Warner Bros. Pictures, 2011.

VanDrunen, David. "Bearing Sword in the State, Turning Cheek in the Church: A Reformed Two-Kingdoms Interpretation of Matthew 5:38-42." *Themelios* 34, no. 3 (2009): 322-334.

Ware, Bruce A. *God's Greater Glory: The Exalted God of Scripture and the Christian Faith*. Wheaton, Ill: Crossway Books, 2004.

SCRIPTURE INDEX

Genesis
1	25, 99
1-2	15, 56, 98
1-3	16
1:1	12, 14, 32
1:26	12, 25, 40, 50, 84
1:28	12
2:7	13
2:18	14
2:20	14
2:24	87
3	7, 16, 25, 42, 57
3:1-6	99-100
3:5	16
3:15	57, 96, 99, 102

Exodus
3:21-22	10-11
12:35-36	10-11
19:5-6	68-69
20:7	33
22:18	30

Numbers
12:1-16	72
12:9	15

Deuteronomy
7:3-4	73-74
18:10	30
32:39	62

Joshua
2	66-69
2:10-12	69
2:11	69
24:19	15

2 Kings
22:13	15

Job
1-2	35
1:8	92
1:9-11	92
1:12	92-93
1:13-19	93
1:21	93
2:1-8	93
2:6	93
2:9	93

Psalms
5:4	62
19:1-6	78-79
99:9	16
119:11	8, 20, 86, 108

139:14	41, 72	**Mark**	
145:8	15	1:14-15	102
		2:5-12	44
Proverbs		2:28	59
9:10	65, 108-109	7:17-23	107-108
		8:36	64
Isaiah		14:21	62
42:5	13	15:34	95
45:7	62	16:6	35
53:4-6	44		
		Luke	
Jeremiah		6:22	51
17:9	55, 107-108	15:1-2	77
		16:22-23	105-106
Matthew		20:34-38	98
1:23	102	22:3	36
4:1-11	99-101, 104	22:31	91
5:10–11	50	23:34	38
5:17	48	23:39-43	105
5:27-28	87	23:43	105-106
5:38-42	47-50		
5:43-44	37	**John**	
5:43-48	38	1:1	13, 14, 33, 102
7:1-2	59-60		
7:1-5	60	1:1-3	45, 46
7:20-24	54	1:4	16
8:28-34	102	1:4-5	62
13:38-39	101	3:16	38, 98, 104
13:38-43	57	4:24	13
15:10-11	6-7	5:17-47	20-21
15:17-20	6-7	5:19	78
18:7	62	7:21-24	59
22:37-39	66	7:24	59
22:37-40	53, 60, 63	8:44	93, 96
22:39	48, 69	10:10	65
22:41-46	104	10:14-18	44
26:36-44	44	10:18	103
26:39	44	12:31-32	101
27:11	102	12:36	98
27:44	106	13:27	99
28:18-20	54, 98	14:2-6	103

THE HARRY POTTER BIBLE STUDY

14:6	8, 20-21, 25, 26, 33, 38, 44, 56, 57, 75	8:19-23	17
		8:20-22	25
		8:28	46-47, 65
		8:31-39	65
14:21, 23	98	10:9-11	8
15:23	96	12:18-21	49
18:36	48-49	12:19	34
		13:1-7	34, 48-51
Acts			
2:23	35-36, 62, 96	**1 Corinthians**	
		6:13	86
3:22-23	102	7:39	73
4:12	102	9:24-27	83
5	90	10:31	41
5:3-4	90	11:1	9
5:5	90	15:1-4	75
5:7-8	90-91	15:55-57	103
5:9-10	91		
5:41	50	**2 Corinthians**	
16:16-18	30-31	5:8-10	105-106
22:25-29	50	5:17-21	49
		5:18	49
Romans		5:20-21	43-44
1	17, 33, 98	5:21	101
2:14-15	16	6:14-16	73-74
3	16	10:5	10, 21, 23
3:10-23	25	12	36
3:23	8, 16, 25, 26, 43, 97, 107-108	12:2-10	46
		Galatians	
5	90	3:22	25, 43
5:8	38, 97-98	5:16-17	82
5:12-21	99, 104	5:19-20	31
6:23	8, 38, 97, 103	5:22-23	57-58
		5:22-25	7-8
7:4	76	5:24	82
8:1-11	38	5:25	82
8:1-39	25		
8:8-11	76	**Ephesians**	
8:9	14, 76	2:1-7	57
8:13	80	2:1-10	57

2:8-9	95
2:11-18	75-76
2:20	90
4:14	94
4:17-24	82
4:29	32-34
5:2	102
5:25	51
6:10-18	80-81

Philippians
2:9-11	61
2:12-13	82-83
4:6	109
4:8	23-24

Colossians
1:16-17	12, 13, 25, 32, 35, 41, 46, 50-51
1:19-22	8
1:21-23	97
2:2-3	33
3:1-10	82
3:17	32

1 Thessalonians
5:20-22	77

1 Timothy
5:18	61

2 Timothy
3:16-17	15, 33, 58

Hebrews
2:14	101
4:15	43
6:20	102
10:31	62-63
11:31	69
13:20	102-103

James
1:26	33
2:14-17	75
3:5-6	33
4:7	80

1 Peter
1:13-16	90
2:20-25	38
3:15	39
3:18	103
4:1-2	49
5:8	42, 91

2 Peter
1:21	58
3:9	15

1 John
1:8-10	43
2:2	44-45
4:10	44-45

Revelation
19:20	57
20:10, 14, 15	57
21	35

ABOUT THE AUTHOR

Jared Moore has served in ministry for 11 years and is currently the pastor of New Salem Baptist Church in Hustonville, KY. He has an M.A.R. in Biblical Studies from Liberty Baptist Theological Seminary, an M.Div. in Christian Ministry from Southern Baptist Theological Seminary, and is currently completing a Th.M. in Systematic Theology at Southern Baptist Theological Seminary. He and his wife, Amber, reside in Hustonville, KY with their two children. If you have any questions or if you are interested in inviting Jared to speak, you may contact him through his website. Jared writes at http://jaredmoore.exaltchrist.com. He is also a contributor at www.sbcvoices.com.

CPSIA information can be obtained at www.ICGtesting.com
Printed in the USA
BVOW02s1845101213

338730BV00001B/46/P